CRYPTOGRAM -A-DAY BOOK

Louise B. Moll

Sterling Publishing Co., Inc.
New York

This book is dedicated to my grandsons, Steven Daniel and Howard Jacob, with love.

Acknowledgments

My sincere thanks to Dr. Jan Tobochnik and Dr. Wesley E. Bramnick, for the computer program and assistance, once again. To Sheila Anne Barry, acquisition director, for her input, vision, and faith in me, and to Hannah Steinmetz, a great editor, for her talent, patience, and sense of humor. You're all the best! How lucky for me.

Library of Congress Cataloging-in-Publication Data

Moll, Louise B.
    Cryptogram-a-day book / Louise B. Moll.
        p.   cm.
    Includes index.
    ISBN 0-8069-8110-5
    1. Cryptograms. I. Title.
    GV1507.C8M646   1996
    793.73–dc20   96-28210
                            CIP

30   29

Published by Sterling Publishing Co., Inc.
387 Park Avenue South, New York, NY 10016
© 1996 by Louise B. Moll
Distributed in Canada by Sterling Publishing
ᶜ/o Canadian Manda Group, 165 Dufferin Street
Toronto, Ontario, Canada M6K 3H6
Distributed in Great Britain and Europe by Chris Lloyd at Orca Book
Services, Stanley House, Fleets Lane, Poole BH15 3AJ, England
Distributed in Australia by Capricorn Link (Australia) Pty. Ltd.
P.O. Box 704, Windsor, NSW 2756, Australia

Sterling ISBN 0-8069-8110-5

For information about custom editions, special sales, premium and corporate purchases, please contact Sterling Special Sales Department at 800-805-5489 or specialsales@sterlingpub.com.

CONTENTS

A Note to Cryptographers

It used to be difficult to find cryptogram books in the stores, but no more. You don't have to rely on the handful of puzzles in crossword puzzle magazines anymore, because my first three books, *The Great Book of Cryptograms, Clever Cryptograms,* and *Baffling Cryptograms,* are in your local bookstores now.

My collections are made up of meaningful thoughts of philosophers and great thinkers, or proverbs that have come down through the ages. In fact, these three books have provided you with 1,180 fun puzzles, which should keep you busy for a while.

Now you're in for a special treat. *Cryptogram-A-Day Book* offers 366 more puzzles, one for each day, not forgetting leap-year babies. After you have checked your birthday message and a few other dates, settle down and do one every day.

So, sharpen those pencils, keep your erasers handy, and get to work! Most of all, enjoy....

How to Use This Book

A cryptogram is a communication in code, using a scrambled alphabet that substitutes one letter for another. Breaking it is an exercise in logic, imagination, and perseverance. Logic, as you search out the patterns and structure of the words and sentences you're trying to uncover. Imagination, as you intuit words from the jumble before you. Perseverance, as you stick with the trial-and-error search.

If you've never solved a cryptogram before, you'll need to know certain facts: Each cryptogram is coded differently, but in any single quotation, the code is consistent. No letter ever stands for itself.

For example, a C could represent an E throughout the message, and an F could be an R.

```
WE'RE    PUZZLED    PUZZLERS
HC'FC    KYNNACP    KYNNACFX
```

The most common three-letter words include *the, and, but, for,* and *are.* Common two-letter words are *it, is, of, in,* and *to.* Long word endings include *ing, ion, est, ied,* and *ally.*

Start by tracking down these telltale patterns, and with the letters you detect, you'll soon clue into other formations that will eventually reveal the message.

The order of frequency of the most used letters in the English language is:

$$E - T - A - O - I - N - S - H - R - D - L - U$$

and it has probably never helped anyone to know that!

Have fun with these crypts!

JANUARY

1 *Answer on page 97*

FXA SRZ YNJIJS UC SRZ YZXYUT
VOXEEZT AUHI RZXIS XTE TUHIJYR
AUHI YUHO.   —OUHJYZ L. FUOO

2 *Answer on page 98*

VLG CJMAFVCJXVG VLUJR XIACV
VLUD QAFTP UD VLXV RAAP
LXIUVD XFG DA OCYL GXDUGF
VA RUZG CW VLXJ IXP AJGD.
         —Q. DAOGFDGV OXCRLXO

3 *Answer on page 98*

GQLOSDCM DR BFWCQSOCH
UHXOQRH SF LOS DR QSGOIIM
HNXHIC UM GDR FPS BOQJC.
         —JQXDQR OSSOHQR RHSHXO

4 *Answer on page 101*

OHJGD YT OJLXB QSYB TYBHGE,
JDA NTEY SNMTGYJDY, JY
ZTLGEHOV.   —VGJDC YZXHG

XQ XP QNV IKCZXMLV CE
WMCRAVSYV QC PIVUW, UMS XQ
XP QNV IKXZXAVYV CE RXPSCD
QC AXPQVM.

—CAXZVK RVMSVAA NCADVP

MUDX, MUPX XCXAH ZKOXA
SMXYYUBQ, LXAUCXY UKY
CNMVX DAZW UKY VYX NMZBX.

—YNWVXM TZOBYZB

EJ JEQ VEJKA KOHR NR NA ROHR
OQ GHE MJ CERNW OQ RSNQA.

—YCXWNCA ALSCA

SR CMR CFF OMCPRFRMK AJ OUR
BRKRMO ZQ FAQR CJB OUR LRKO
SR NCJ QAJB AJ ZTM HZTMJRG
AK CJ UZJRKO QMARJB.

—MZLRMO FZTAK KORPRJKZJ

DPBBAWGFF AF WMC CDG

FCPCAMW YG PNNAQG PC SVC

CDG ZPWWGN SU YDAXD YG

PNNAQG.   —MIAQGN H. YAIFMW

K NKUN NVEWVU PVXVU

EVQQAMC MLNY KTV, KPH K

CYKUW NAPTDV LC NYV APQB

VHTVH NAAQ NYKN TUAMC

FVVPVU MLNY ZAPCNKPN DCV.

—MKCYLPTNAP LUXLPT

ZEJJSZZ GNSZ RNB JNRZQZB QR

RSDSA ICPQRH VUERGSAZ, VEB QR

RSDSA ICPQRH BFS ZCIS NRS BFS

ZSJNRG BQIS. —FSRAX TFSSUSA ZFCT

EG EC SNZWOUFTC GF YO CEZHOUO

TZDOCC RFT NUO NDCF CGTBES.

—WOFUWO YOUZNUS CINX

LFTDV YFT ATCLVBRKSLV LFV

WVSELQ TG LFV VSULF GXCH

UVDVUJVD TG DLUVCZLF LFSL

YXKK VCHEUV SD KTCZ SD KXGV

KSDLD.   —USAFVK ASUDTC

YB LE UZD ZUKS LPKB IYZ PZBE

UZDYLUO, XTD YB LE LPKB IYZ

CLOYD XB XBDDBJ BCHKZSBP.

                    —EZNJRDBE

BR OQEX QER XYOR DIRGXYWRSP

GVM JTIRWRI IRGSYKR XNGX XNR

XYOR YE GSBGPE IYCR XT MT

IYHNX.—OGIXYV SQXNRI LYVH, UI.

OHMPHBH KTUK MPRH PL EGXKT

MPBPCQ UCF NGVX OHMPHR

EPMM THMA DXHUKH KTH RUDK.

                    —EPMMPUW SUWHL

NVK QYUVN BFQA ZCP RK

KWWKXNYJK, RON HF BFQA BCI

KJKQ CI KWWKXNYJK CI C

QYUVNDP NYZKA SCOIK.

—ZCQT NBCYH

N TND PRG JMYFSC RYTCSQI GD

RYC NDKSCVMW YC QYLS VRS

JGVNVG JQNDV, VRS OSCV JNMV

GI PRYKR YC XDFSMUMGXDF.

—CJNDYCR JMGHSMO

AEANW LCJZQY FMJ QXLA MX

ALLAXZNRLRZW; AEANW RUAM

FMJ QXLA MX MKJCNURZW.

—VQGKNQQT PMLTJQX

VLDAD CG YZVLCYI ND ADEDCKD

NCVL GZ QXEL ADOXEVUYED UG

UJKCED.   —MZGDWL UJJCGZY

UJ BKKJOQCZMI ASDBU UIZXAM,
YD OHMU XJU JXCE BKU FHU
BCMJ WSDBO, XJU JXCE QCBX
FHU BCMJ FDCZDPD.

    —BXBUJCD LSBXKD

UOLHL GD BMRBKD AXL WAWLXU
GX NOGMIOAAI ROLX UOL IAAH
AYLXD BXI MLUD UOL QCUCHL
GX.   —PHBOBW PHLLXL

MT JRZ OR FRE ECHH EXC EYZEX
VDRZE JRZYGCHT, JRZ KVFFRE
ECHH ME VDRZE REXCY NCRNHC.

    —LMYIMFMV URRHT

HKZLTB LO H KUXC LW IYB
VHUPBI; IYB OXAADS HDQHSO
BMTBBKO IYB KBVHWK.

    —RNOY FLDDLWCO

25

Answer on page 119

KJ KW DTWKDP JL VKOQJ VLP
LGD'W UPKGMKUSDW JQTG JL
SKBD ZU JL JQDN.

—TSVPDR TRSDP

26

Answer on page 120

MENDYI K XDI BHEYZMQ DJ
NDSG BHHSDYI K JCKNN VDJF.
ZHH CEBF FKYLNDYI TDNN
JOHDN DZ.   —NKH ZUE

27

Answer on page 121

WBAN JI O TWNOIJSP VBWWZ;
ORXJLJBS JI O INCJBHI
ILHTJEJLZ. —SJUBWOI UGORVBCL

28

Answer on page 124

IUPZ ATUAVT SUNVJ PNRRTTJ KY
PICVV ZOKYMP KB ZOTF STGT
YUZ ZGUNHVTJ SKZO MGTCZ
CIHKZKUYP.   —OTYGF SCJPSUGZO
                VUYMBTVVUS

BVRJR GJR BVJRR WPKJRXWRPBT

WP BVR KQQX MWLR: MRGJPWPK,

RGJPWPK GPX NRGJPWPK.

—IVJWTBQOVRJ YQJMRN

LOQTOY GUT CYYKR XUY

LFWPWXQ XT RYY FYLMXQ

OYHYE SETGR TPI.

—NELOB CLNCL

NLSSKEJMM KM HAAC IAF QNJ

GACB, GPQ MAFFAV

MQFJEHQNJEM QNJ MSKFKQ.

—ULFXJW SFAPMQ

FEBRUARY

1 *Answer on page 97*

MWIP OD AWC HMPBP QWN SOYP
LNC HMPBP CMPQ NAJPBDCZAJ
QWN. —RMBODCOZA IWBTPADCPBA

2 *Answer on page 98*

OFZL FD BGL MUB KZ QUMVFRS
DIZZFNFLRB NKRNOIDFKRD ZUKE
FRDIZZFNFLRB CULEFDLD.
                    —DMEILO HIBOLU

3 *Answer on page 99*

YZUR BKT ZUFTQX FTU UHVQL,
YU DBAAUDQ QZWRMX.
            —IWOOZK STWXZRFHKTQW

4 *Answer on page 122*

U PULAGH JK U CGBBYS SDY
BGLVK ZYT DJK TNPHGBBU SDGL
FDG KTL JK KDJLJLQ ULV SULFK
JF PUMA FDG NJLTFG JF PGQJLK
FY HUJL.   —NUHA FSUJL

5

Answer on page 100

YX YD AZNNV XZ FGKFBEZH XZ
CBIF ZWHDFNEFD DLYGF TFAZHF
SF BHF NWCYGZWD.

—LZHBPF TWDLGFNN

6

Answer on page 101

VIO COUV YMS VJ DJRAKRDO M
BJJX VIMV IO KU YLJRW KU VJ
XOV IKE IMAO IKU JYR YMS.

—QJUI CKXXKRWU

7

Answer on page 113

BKM XODA EKVDAUVV DV ABF FB
VUU TYOF ZDUV HDXZS OF O
HDVFOAIU, EKF FB HB TYOF
ZDUV IZUOMZS OF YOAH.

—FYBXOV IOMZSZU

8

Answer on page 103

ARH HPH LO ARH JLUQMJ MY
ARH OMBD; ARH LUAHDDHXA
VUQ JLDD VWH OHHU LU LA.

—RLWVK NMJHWO

C GCV QIM ICT VNLNF ONNV SV
ACVDNF RCVVMB CVTQNF JMF
IST RMWFCDN. —JFCVRMST AN ZC
FMRINJMWRCWZA

RO RK OCYQDZC OCI GYEGUK RM
QDY JYERMK OCEO IGKOEKP
GYIIFK RM.
—XQZEM FIEYKEXX KVROC

PWWJW JD JRGMGJM OHQ XP
CJEPWHCPN KVPM WPHAJM GA
EPDC DWPP CJ YJOXHC GC.
—CVJOHA FPDDPWAJM

WLH OHNW WLRTF IOKSW WLH
BSWSEH RN WLIW RW MKDHN
KTGV KTH AIV IW I WRDH.
—IOEILID GRTMKGT

13

Answer on page 108

LR EDB NZCX XD UVV NTZX
ITLQSKVC IZC SD, EDB HBUX
UXDF ALGLCA XTVH XTLCAU.

     —CDKHZC SDBAQZU

14

Answer on page 109

TSOB CSHYWA MC YSSQ, XHA
YMOBG HGCSHYWA MC XBAABI.

     —UMTTMPL CWPNBCVBPIB

15

Answer on page 110

FGY JCGRU URNCJZ XYE YBJCRYN
FBUG; SBFGY JCGRU URNCJZ XYE
YBJCRYN QGZZ. —ZHZXY P. XYJCBYA

16

Answer on page 104

ZHWT DK LJT SDKMHG HN LJT
NHHZ OYM LJT NHZZI HN LJT
SDKT.   —KOGETZ AHJYKHY

17

Answer on page 105

W YLWVVS IOBS MLYBPU ULJLY
HUPDB NPD COAN NL DLZRNB.

     —LFRWY DWQBPU NPDL

VEKNK JW YU PXNK RUN SJNVE
UN MKBVE KZPKOV VU KYTUH
VEK JYVKNLBD.

—IKUNIK WBYVBHBYB

OT TOI ADO PJRVK URM
MIAJHRNZ JSTO NUI OTPVIOIMM
TW DOTNUIH SIHMTO.

—XRVVD ADNUIH

ZYXTX BF OCZ WJX FCOFZBZCZX
GWT BUIKBJIZBWJ, IJM ZYIZ BF
XNLXTBXJHX.

—KXDXZZX OCTKXFF

USP LBS SPJPX LUSRPSO OU
LXPPN YZPS USP DPPAR BS
QWNIARP OU RUBX.

—ZPAPS VPAAPX

V XCDA ZXJ BEUVB FC DJQQ

EMMDVPERDJ ZC MORDVP ZXEF

ZC MTVYEZJ ESSEVTQ, ZXEZ

XCFJQZK VQ EDHEKQ ZXJ RJQZ

MCDVPK.   —IJCTIJ HEQXVFIZCF

VQC JKCPV TICPNAKC DU IDLC

DN MBDUJ GQPV TCBTIC NPF FBA

SPUUBV MB.   —GPIVCK RPJCQBV

RQJHGN NFQJZC HQJ XTQ YMJ

NSDQDY IMHY NZJJS DN XTQ

YMJ ATRC. —XQDJRQDEM MJAAJZ

JCM SMUVSI FY V JCNPX UMKK

IFPM NL JF CVWM IFPM NJ.

        —SVKZC UVKIF MDMSLFP

J KJC NF JF HBBU JF IA IJF ZB
DA, JCU J QBKJC JF DJU JF FIA
UJTAF.   —AVDATZ IODDJTU

XZBFFLJX JEL IGOKBNI ZIBDLDQX
BFI KAQIKR NL HFIBQ B NEAVE.
                    —HOFGIXI ZFLWIFH

RZCTRGOCRO GT E BZXLOW-GC-
DEQ QLZTO UGTGX COUOW OCAT.
                    —L. D. BOCRSOC

CFLUE HTLBQL THTW IYXC JBQ
LXFO JBQ ZFLJ XI QDQYWZTW
OUIQ.   —PQYJBXOZ TFQYPTEB

MARCH

QKHEF SFPCMD PCDPMQR WCG

REUTFWCYT; PFECV W GTTBTF WCG

UTDD AFPTCGUV KCGTFDRWCGPCM.

             —WMCTD FTBBUPTF

CT OP MTACPAC EWCQ XWCCXP

WG QVZH, CT OP MTACPAC EWCQ

DNMQ WDKTGGWOXP.

             —DVZWP FTA POAPZ

                PGMQPAOVMQ

OL VR LXKFCILX POE DWEPR

POLGL IE NVWX EKI POCI OL

XELRW'I DWEP.   —YLEGY RVHHLB

VCA FVLJ EFHVAJBXJ JWVCOWJL

BAU JWVLU NWEZW ZVXJABKEZJ

VCA UFVJEVXL.   —HBCY IBYUAQ

VMA XIBSSAXV NAASRUTX BOA

HEOVM IEOA VMBU VMA IEXV

GABPVRNPS VMEPTMVX.

—GAOUBOW WA NEUVAUASSA

RZGIG UC K RULG RD JUOB KC

JGVV KC RD CGG.

—RZDLKC WAVVGI

G YESL JHGDV EU G NBOSVGES

BN WMGLSHUU, AGYESW

HQHDPVJESW ES EVU QEFESEVP

NDHUJHS ESVB UAEMHU.

—IGUJESWVBS EDQESW

DQ BWX SWE'H CEWY YVRUR

BWX'UR OWDEO, JEB TJHV YDAA

HJCR BWX HVRUR.

—MDWXF TUWGRUN

9

Answer on page 104

MSUMTBMIKM BJ IFO CAGO
AGUUMIJ OF WFV; BO BJ CAGO
WFV NF CBOA CAGO AGUUMIJ OF
WFV.   —GXNFVJ AVSXMW

10

Answer on page 105

DWB ABBYBTD YGJLSJYVB NE
WCZHL LHDCGB JT DWB SGHKJLU
DN IB HYYGBSJHDBA.

               —FJVVJHZ MHZBT

11

Answer on page 106

XR XBZGXJRAXRBL AQXA ELCJRD
YJAQ X BISMNJSLRA JD DGVL AI
FLPLNIM JRAI X VLXN
HVJLRFDQJM.   —IDBXV YJNFL

12

Answer on page 108

VPHSQE LQWHPHJH PW YRPWM
IYTR JQ SPHJPWMBPHX IEQWM
SIWMRZH IWS EINR I LXQPLR QD
JXR TRIHJ XIZEDBT.

          —WPLLQTQ EILXPIKRTTP

RUCDCRDH PKDDRQ HBGXCXA CT

RDA IKH DR PIKDPA QR TCJIQ

TRG QIAY. —QIRYKH YKDD

AURJLJDWV LT JMV NRLUVTJ

XKETTEF YMLSM THULQAT NUEF

JMV TEDK.

—MVQUC YRUW XVVSMVU

WGMF VJGVZJ VRF GYY FDZZ

FGWGQQGI FLHF ILDAL FLJU

MLGRZP LHXJ PGOJ UJMFJQPHU.

—JPCHQ IHFMGO LGIJ

ZVJK SK ESO DTJJ RF XJIIJY, DVJ

ZVEIJ XETJFD JGVEJF ZRDV RD,

ACD S VCKYTJY SGETKF STJ

UISKDJY FRIJKDIP AP FEBJ

CKFJJK XETGJ. —DVEBSF GSTIPIJ

AMAPO DHCRXVMP EMV RVYVM

DHCRXVMP WK UOV OVEMU.

—TEMAE VXLVZWMUO

DFTBXGTT PXR SBCG POG SBHG P

DPXH PEEZFXK. LZF EPX'K KPHG

ZFK JZOG KUPX LZF QFK BX.

—IBSSBPJ CGPKUGO

QM QZ NCJP BFNBJF NU ZGDJJ

GNODJ ZMDMVOF XSN SDWF MN

ZMDCH NC MSFQO HQICQMP.

—DOCNJH KFCCFMM

HEKPAUUFEKU CGL VA DEEQ PEY

WNA UEZJ VZW WNAL GYA VGQ

PEY WNA YAIZWGWFEK.

—JEYQ QABGY

XQG RYYB ALK EP QLRRF; QG

GIRGOXP KY OQLKNG TYB XQG

VYBPG.   —CGAGXBEZP

WLWK Y DAIV XMCRSK'N ZWN

AKNM NBMCPRW AD AN EWQN

ANI FMCNV IVCN.

                    —EMBWYK QBMLWBP

PZY PGT MSYKPYNP NPHFQEKVPN

HV PZY GTSEO KSY WTQPZ KVO

OYLP.   —LYVRKFHV OHNSKYEH

QFYJOHIKYT WDOIYIUI YO

QDFVJUUYOV ZKCU DOJ VYXJI,

COH FJBJBNJFYOV ZKCU DOJ

FJWJYXJI.

                —CEJMCOHFJ HABCI (TJFJ)

25

HAL XFUCK QP RJCC FR XQCCQTS

DLFDCL; PFGL XQCCQTS HF

XFUM, HAL ULPH XQCCQTS HF

CLH HALG.   —UFILUH RUFPH

26

YBQ YO AGQ KTQCAQFA VHQIQF

YO QIYBYSHI EHFXYS HF AY LBYE

EGCA PYM XY BYA LBYE.

          —RYGB LQBBQAG KCNJTCHAG

27

QFW YWNQ TZK QG XWQ GO CO

QFW TGVDI CN QG RZSW

UWGUDW YWDCWEW CQ'N QG

QFWCV ZIEZOQZXW QG FWDU

KGH.   —LWZO IW DZ YVHKWVW

28

EXU IRILMUBSEZ UBFU SD CXLI

HSOOSWAJU SD CXLI

CILSUXLSXAD.

          —DU. UBXCFD FVASEFD

JZ ZJA AIAD FAXNSA
RLZDZQPLMU FNK HJ ZJA ERAT.

—OQIAJNM

MXQR FV YJL DQLIYLVY YJFPD
FP YJL MXQNS, VX ML VJXHNS
INMIEV VIKL VXTL XG FY GXQ
YXTXQQXM.   —SXP JLQXNS

WBD TDEYZGD FC E TEH'Y GDEA
LBEGELWDG UY PBEW BD PFZAR
RF UC BD VHDP BD HDNDG
PFZAR OD CFZHR FZW.

—WBFTEY OEOUHKWFH TELEZAEJ

APRIL

AX ZSS TCH'E TVECBVCE LWC
GVLLCBCEL VE LA UHAY EA TQJW
ZHI LA WZMC JAHLBAS AMCB
HALWVHK.   —WCBAIALQE

JWKNNKH RQK GLKZ FLB LRYK
UBGLXUI GB NRZ, RUH FLB
SRUUBG JK TKQNARHKH GB NRZ
XG.   —ERVKN QANNKWW WBFKWW

QFT SATYQ KTOATQ NP MCPT CK
RTUTA QN ET CR QFT BYG NP
NQFTAK.   —QFNJYK OFYRHMTA
                          FYMCEIAQNR

JESGW PNIDH E CEF JPY GWI
RDQIYHGEDQSDL; RDXITSIJ
ATPHIH SG.   —HG. ERLRHGSDI

5

Answer on page 100

QP DWDBM QIFGK QIDBD FN X
NDXNPG, XGC X QFTD QP DWDBM
UZBUPND ZGCDB QID IDXWDG.

—DSSYDNFXNQDN

6

Answer on page 108

B CHOLOBNL SGJLPN FLBGZ
VHPTLG YCBP HPL UHD XDU JP
YCL OBGWLY. —BDZYJP H'OBVVLU

7

Answer on page 102

YGV GTSXQ GVXCY MB NMRV
GVXOVQ; YGV SJCV XQPVNB YGV
SJCV CJJS. —UCVWCMRX LCVSVC

8

Answer on page 105

SD ST OMQC TNHWF DR RZWB DCNP
DR FMGW. —DCRONT N VWOEST

9

Answer on page 104

WYWTMZSHAQ GNDWE ZN SHD
LSN SXEZCWE LSHCW SW LPHZE.

—ZSNDPE PCYP WKHENA

10

Answer on page 103

HWBSZHL ZM MW KTHLVAWCM TM
TH ZLHWATHB NAZVHK; T XZMV
VHVEP ZM GVBBVA.

—OVTH KV QT NWHBTZHV

11

Answer on page 106

PIMXM WN WF IKDYF FYPKXM
CMFMXYHHB DAXM AR PIM RAAH
PIYF AR PIM OWNM.

—RXYFLWN EYLAF

12

Answer on page 111

ZFIP GD OEJIT GD ZFIP HEY KCCT
LEEU IKPCJ, IWU ZFIP GD
GOOEJIT GD ZFIP HEY KCCT XIU
IKPCJ.   —CJWCDP FCOGWLZIH

13

Answer on page 101

CD BCJB UTQDQ CVQ
PTYQPVDYPD CJQ YTBCVYH
UDOB BCJB VQ NTFBC IDDSVYH.

—VAJJI NJUBTY

ROU ME SRR KO PSGGZ STB RJYO
DJUPJT FMQ VOSTE, OYOT JL DO
PSYO UF KFQQFD UPO VFTOZ UF
BF JU DJUP.   —SQUOVME DSQB

FRGKX KJ BQT AZOBQ LQTO BQT
YGTTO GTBPGOJ BZ BQT XFLO,
BQT BGTTJ FON BQT KOBTGOFX
GTETOPT JTGEKVT.   —TEFO TJFG

RK RP ZLPRN'P CFJKB ZRPPRFQ
KF PGUY CRTGK FQ KGU YUHKGP
FJ KGU GLZEQ GUEAK.

                —AFVUΛK PNGLZEQQ

FUKPA HI DHOP V IHCQL IPKIP
XHQLUTQ XLHGL AUT GVKKUQ
FVOP V GUFJDPQP TIP UZ QLP
UQLPN ZHBP.

            —X. IUFPNIPQ FVTWLVF

18

Answer on page 113

AQZ'K ZFCYBQK FBQ FTDRQ; DC
DK CIQDB IFXDCK CIFC NFBBE
CIQA GFB FSFBC.   —NUZGYNDYK

19

Answer on page 114

GCRR UC ZQFG KVUWFXS SVH
ICCW, FXP D'RR GCRR SVH ZQFG
SVH FJC.—UDNHCR PC KCJYFXGCL

20

Answer on page 115

UFYV KITPNVY WIHYJ, JYASY FYT
AV PFY KTIVP UAPF M JNTY
FMVG, EYWMNJY EYFAVG JFY AJ
EMBG.   —BYIVMTGI GM DAVWA

21

Answer on page 116

NZBT B LXBPLV BPY FEH IEP'M
TV OEZZF CEZ B GSNXM-XBUV-
TVVP.   —BZMXHZ ZBPOEGV

22

Answer on page 120

SUPC UJ ALL JTLOA AL DC
SUAASC.   —DCYVNGUY EUJONCSU

23

Answer on page 118

GOMBSOQQS NOQXN WOA TPC PN
TQDCMCE NOQXN WOA SPV.

—FQOC TMBWQC

24

Answer on page 119

TCYYCD TC ZOTUDO YXWO
ZOYWZHXY, BUD QHOUDWOKC QL
YXC DUUY UB EQLBUDYZOC.

—MJWYU

25

Answer on page 117

LFEMXP RUFP JQWA MA TXPA,
WER AWSFEA RUFP JQWA MA IWE.

—UJFE TFBFRMAQ

26

Answer on page 120

TSS WFI PITBUJQJEB UC ZIJ TPI
JUW GUPWF UJI BIJWQZIJW UC
GUZIJ.   —YUSWTQPI

27

Answer on page 112

FA SUH'W EZUF UOSAZ, FA EZUF
ZCDAZ.   —DLJOU DCGLTTU

28

Answer on page 121

OMNL AMN PUDLG UNHG AMN

PUDLG, LQ OQLGNJ AMNV PQAM

BHUU DLAQ YHAJDYQLV.

—ENQJEN BHJSKMHJ

29

Answer on page 123

AH N DNG FJRQI LNYO LNQH LAW

TAWLOW, LO TJRQI IJRPQO LAW

VXJRPQOW.

—POGBNDAG HXNGUQAG

30

Answer on page 124

YITMCKM NT PZ UZBM ARYP

ANCX NT PZ QNLM; NP

MOPNCSHNTRMT PRM TDYUU, NP

NCQUYDMT PRM SLMYP.

—KZDPM XM IHTTJ-LYIHPNC

MAY

1 *Answer on page 97*

MOJ'Q XJPS SRLJ RQ QM MLWJO

WBJ SRLJ WBPW MOJ KMJQ OMW

SJPK.   —MQYPX VRSKJ

2 *Answer on page 98*

LDJ RCLJ PR MPBJ UX LDCL UL

CMICNX XJJYX LPP MULLMJ PA

LPP YEHD.   —CYJMUC TCAA

3 *Answer on page 102*

WAZ VCDRVPVWU WK HWDU

OIVZW VH KCZ KL WAZ XKHW

FKCHSVFIKIH LDVPVCMH KL

XDCNVCG.   —BDPWZE RDMZAKW

4 *Answer on page 104*

ZOZDREBZ WENVUPCBL EH XCL

NZNEDR, PBI BE EBZ WENVUPCBL

EH XCL MJIQNZBA.

          —HDPBWECL IZ UP

          DEWXZHEJWPJUI

5

ZFK OEZZOK HSDVOKMQK ZFLZ

LIZX EX VDTZF ESAESEZKOB

JDTK ZFLS JRIF HSDVOKMQK

ZFLZ EX EMOK. —HLFOEO QECTLS

6

FMGYXNXI ND GX QYXGVMXA NX

WYQDWMYNAE, G YMHBIM NX

GULMYDNAE, GXU G WYQLNDNQX

NX QFU GIM.   —GYNDAQAFM

7

FIL RUM KUPFLR CZ CFILWP QP

ZCF KUPFLR CZ CZLPLTO.

                —GIUWTLP RQGXLZP

8

XTLWL ON GAXTOGF NA GOUL RN

IAOGF FAAI DB NXLRHXT RGI

DLOGF JAQGI AQX DB RUUOILGX.

                —UTRWHLN HRYD

FBQQEJLPP EP B VHPDLXH, IESL
XLIENEYJ, BJG PFYOIG JLZLX CL
XBDEYJBIERLG.—N. S. WFLPDLXDYJ

WGZCJ JDXOWDJY GZMOHZM JX
FGCHJSHZ KZHXLZ WGZCJ CHJY.

　　　　　　　　—NSPPSCL DCUPSJJ

YRC ONWXA HYKVAH NW GKXXH
ODYR YRC XKOH NG XDGC
ORDMR RCKPCV RKH OWDYYCV
DV YRC RJFKV MNVHMDCVMC.

　　　　　　　　—ZDCWWC PKV ZKKHHCV

OCD QHHVZTC GKY TDDST
CKFFZYDTT ZY OCD LZTOKYID;
OCD PZTD BUHPT ZO WYLDU CZT
QDDO.　　　—AKGDT HFFDYCDZG

13

Answer on page 102

UWK RKLRKUZTX SDIUTPXK US
WZOTF TEATFPKOKFU BI PZIUSO.

—HSWF IUZTLU OBXX

14

Answer on page 113

I SBAXTW YX ABIZZL IZYUB
TWZL EPBW PB YX OTUYWK
DTAEIAN VT XTOBVPYWK OTAB.

—EYWDABN APTNBX

15

Answer on page 118

ZKUZ KGYE SW FIBMYJ
UHHGEZUMYG QKSHK JIB IAAGN
WEIXZUXGIBWYJ QKGX QG
WZUXF SX XGGF.

—EBMYSBW WJNBW

16

Answer on page 123

WNFW LT WKV LDWVYCYVWVY MI
NJJ YLEEJVT, WKV TSYBMSDWVY
MI NJJ ELIILFSJWLVT, WKV
YVBMHVY MI NJJ MPTWNFJVT.

—RLJJLNB TFNYZLJJ

17

Answer on page 106

ECY ZJK FE FTK LRCKZURKY VH
GVRFKU; FE FTK CKZURKY VF VH
TZUQKHF FVOK.

    —PLYZT CKVX CZNKUEQ

18

Answer on page 109

ICP WDMH RPDTZDP XWSFDBP
NWX RXWED QPWQMP ZK
XPFMZIH.   —ICWSFK BFXMHMP

19

Answer on page 114

AO ZIM LFZZRM BQD
MCAKZMOGM, ZFRMOZ AK ZIM
JTOGI, FOY ZFGZ AK ZIM
GRMWMD BQQZ XQDH.

    —XARKQO SANOMD

20

Answer on page 115

FDQNQ GNQ, LM QOQNP GIQ,
MQT QNNANX FA EQ NQRFLBLQK,
GMK MQT SNQCYKLRQX FA EQ
ASSAXQK.   —XGVYQJ CADMXAM

21

Answer on page 116

XHK AUKW OUS JXPK GW
BFCQACWF, XW RKURQK WXE; CS
UOQE VCOAW GW WSCQQ SYGK
BFCQAYKO. —DUFXOO NUQVHXOH
IUO HUKSFK

22

Answer on page 117

FGKWMYBEARGK MKYRFVMB AVM
HKCMYBAEKCRKN, IHA
BGTRAHCM RB AVM BFVGGT GQ
NMKRHB. —MCPEYC NRIIGK

23

Answer on page 110

HAJ QSYVOJYH QW V AQGUJ CU
HAJ WSCJYNU EAQ WSJPGJYH CH.
—SVKXA EVKNQ JOJSUQY

24

Answer on page 119

H JEZCL OACLEZC UABK AW
UEFFEOKG TJ HR EFG HMK
OACLEZC KSXKBAKRYK.
—YLHBFKW YHFKT YEFCER

LUKP LK DMK IADPPQPY BRM
IRNWKMQWS, LK RCYUW WR
MKTKTGKM WUDW JQMWCK QN
PRW UKMKHQWDMS.

                    —WURTDN IDQPK

H PFKKIEWRM WV GWDJ H VQWB;
JTJLMFEJ FIZQR RF AJ BLJBHLJS
RF RHDJ RQJ QJGK.

                    —QJELWD WAVJE

FU JHBX RMTBXGTXNE IHYNL
LYQUB MO RMHWGPU XM CMNL
IGRQ XCU ONMML MO OUGW.

        —JGWXYT NHXCUW QYTP, KW.

VBQQJ EC VS HVT VBC
CNUUSSLSL EI FSBDIEIP WVS
UBNCSC TG WVEIPC.   —YEDPEF

BGGH UGNDJCF, EZXF NZRF
UNJZD, GJBTD DG SF FCMGKFH
ITZEF ZD ZW RNFWFCD.

— FRZLDFDJW

SIW FQU UYNYZ PQNY Q
CZYQMYZ IZ Q KYHHYZ OIVJUJIU
MPQU INYZ SIWZHYKD.

— KYIUQZOI OQ NJUFJ

HE DGIGHR SFGHR GC KFDW SL
MHLQKGHR CE CQPEHRDL MC
GQC EUH HFFWC.   — FBGXQFQTC

JUNE

1 *Answer on page 97*

RCMFLWI DFTWLWKW FB RYTVLTV
FT FTC ILTJKC XFTVCM.

—TFMOCVLYT QMFECMN

2 *Answer on page 98*

SMKWKIKW BMK CWB PG
UKVRTRQK RN APIKV, BMKWK
CANP RN APIK PG MDUCQRBF.

—MRZZPTWCBKN

3 *Answer on page 99*

XFHDH QDH XJG VQWI QPGEX
JFYNF ZGPGVW IFGEAV HMHD
JGDDW, QZV XFHIH QDH
WHIXHDVQW QZV XGTGDDGJ.

—DGPHDX SGZHI PEDVHXXH

4 *Answer on page 100*

PDH MHVP PZXH PN WN C PDZLK
ZV ADHL ZP GCL MH WNLH.

—AZEEZCX UZGTHLV

5

Answer on page 101

FTFHK DBX OJYLIQ ZFFU B

PBMH-OMCFQ GFDFWFHK MX

AJMGJ WY ELHK WJF PBLIWO YP

JMO PHMFXQO.

—JFXHK ABHQ EFFGJFH

6

Answer on page 102

QZ XQG QFV LYB GOZ ZOZJK

VQFWW JZZB QMJ ZUZPKXQZPZ.

—GJFP SQFKKFJ

7

Answer on page 105

MATGT PB SNFNQC BN

PGGPMKMPSL KB BNDTFNQC

RPMA ITBB PSMTIIPLTSET KSQ

DNGT BTSBT MAKS RT AKUT.

—QNS ATGNIQ

8

Answer on page 104

JBL KTDL YD VX VUNLXJIWLW TE

JBL OWVGJTGL YD JBL VWJ YD

JBL TSOYEETRKL.

—CTKKTVS RYKTJBY

9

Answer on page 103

LV LB VCX HPOBX BCPAX UH
HUUOB KCLGC VJLXB VU GUWXJ
MICXPOXE BUJXB.   —CUJPGX

10

Answer on page 105

UE UM N RHCCZ ETUCW NSFHE
XURI; UR ZFH KIRHMI EF NJJIGE
NCZETUCW SHE ETI SIME ZFH
YIKZ FREIC WIE UE.

—A. MFOIKMIE ONHWTNO

11

Answer on page 110

NA GZNDPTCZX AQGZGTI CQ NXG
YABTJ, AQG JAGZ DTT AQG MDQ
NA ZGGH GZNDPTCZXGJ NXGBG
DTBGDJR.   —IBDQMACZ JG TD
BAMXGIASMDSTJ

12

Answer on page 107

UOKVZ EH MII UOY LYMSUQ
UOMU'D DUKII IYHU KV MVP
MGESVP QES MVP LY OMNNQ.

—MVVY HGMVZ

13

Answer on page 108

OJN KATO UKYAQOEIO

UISQNZUNIO AP OJN PBOBQN UT

OJN YQNTNIO. —SNAQSN DNAIEQZ

14

Answer on page 109

VOPSP DW RUVODRB VOHV

QUWVW ZPWW VOHR QDYDZDVA.

—TUR FMDKUVP

15

Answer on page 106

SPCTU XTFGNQP OYP UNFG, KAO

OZ JFLP AD PGOYAUFCUR XTFGNQPU

OYP UZAQ.   —UCRAPQ AQQRCG

16

Answer on page 115

KH BRHHAFC YPH SPQ CBRMM HSA

IAZKYYKYZ BRX CAAB HP IA; QSRH

KC PYVA QAMM NPYA KC NPYA

UPFAGAF. —SAYFX NRGKN HSPFARL

17

Answer on page 116

JXLC XG B LJVZCK VL ZSXDS JVHC

XG ASC SVUCT.   —HXDAVK SWRV

OXK NURRMK DA OXK ZDQR UW

VXKZK OXK VXUOK MUCK UW,

QCR OXQO'W OXK VDZWO GMQIK

OD RZUEK.　　—ZDPKZO AZDWO

AJ SN CKXA CN XDN, XGV AJ

SNQJON CKXA CN XDN QXBXSTN

JU SNQJOYGM, YH AKN JGTF NGV

JU TYUN.

　　—DJSNDA TJRYH HANINGHJG

PCSU RV RG H DESGVRZU ZM

OZUSK, SXSNKLZIK RG ZM VCS

GHOS NSFRTRZU.　　—XZFVHRNS

CUWF UJ FDX WDHIUBW UJ FDGW

SGJX HYX THQWXI NA WFHZIGZM

GZ UQY UBZ WQZWDGZX.

　　—YHSED BHSIU XCXYWUZ

22

Answer on page 121

JAC SCEJ TWF JI YBCWEC IDC

AWBM IM JAC TIKBG UE DIJ JI

XUDG TAWJ JAC IJACK AWBM

EWFE. —IBURCK OIBGEXUJA

23

Answer on page 122

DECKYRUMCB CU AMK UMIRWJ

WD AMK KLKYCYF, JMCXM

UAEKYFAMKYU JCAM AMK

UKAACYF UPY WD QCDK.

—VKIY RK QI DWYAICYK

24

Answer on page 119

ZCQO GSCRE SC ZBIBA AC BAE

OSVHYPSLO, SC OSV AC BAE AYHEA,

SC TPVBSN CT BAE WCJO; BA LPS

CHAZPEA PSKAWBSN. —EA. JPHZ

25

Answer on page 120

JIW IHDBWOJ JILFT JQ PWHDF LF

PLRW LO CILMI UDLBTW JQ

MDQOO HFB CILMI JQ UKDF.

—BHSLB DKOOWPP

ZVHP DPVGLLE, XPH OXDSRT
HNHFERVJPB; ZVHP VGLLE XPH
OXDSRT PXRVJPB.—MXTHLV FXDW

LS LH PRDRT SMM AESR SM CR
KUES IMX ZLBUS UEDR CRRP.

—BRMTBR RALMS

XPRBR QBR JRWRBQV LYYH
IBYXRMXCYAJ QLQCAJX
XRKIXQXCYA, SZX XPR JZBRJX CJ
MYTQBHCMR.   —KQBE XTQCA

SVQA SX YXX JXWXZJY PQTZOR IZ
SVQA SX OIIN HIU. —BIVZ OMFFIGN

LRQ HYKOW SP POXFL CSZQ OF SBX
OKVSXYVWQ LRYL OL WYV QZQX
QVI.   —GQVDYHOV IOFXYQCO

JULY

1 *Answer on page 97*

BZ EL RLLU MXL YQLIRGTL FZ

QFNL, YIRRBFS RXFGQH OL

FPPIRBFSIQ, ISH PFDDFS RLSRL

PFSMBSGIQ. —TFOLTMRFS HINBLR

2 *Answer on page 98*

ZW RZTR TNXTPF ECOWF XTP RY

YRZWVF XCNN WJU CJ ZTOCJE JY

AVCJLCANWF YB ZCF YXJ. —TWFYA

3 *Answer on page 99*

WA VWTV YTCVN DSCAH, DATCN,

TCP QSCVACV UN YUVWSXV

VWLAA BSSP GLUACPN.

    —YUEEUTD NWTJANIATLA

4 *Answer on page 100*

RJRHS CMWDRVS GMQMHC DVC

NDJR WMQKMHADCVC BQU DVC

URBU VHMTFNRABORHC.

    —ADIQMQ AWNBTIGNDQ

X C Z F T I V O   W U V   D C F W P Q V   F W P A D :
T W F   M F V N M E Z V F F   X C Z F T F W F   T Z
W U V   P L T E T W J   W C   F W T X S   W C   C Z V
W U T Z Q   W T E E   T W   Q V W F   W U V O V .

—K C F U   L T E E T Z Q F

M G P   M O   U B P   S Z P H U P F U   F M A Z Y P F
M O   F A O O P Z K G S   K F   U M   B H N P   H G
K G C M Z G   F P G F P   M O   B M G M Z .

—C .   I P Y H F F P Z P F

Q V   F I S Z   P V V G   Y B Z   V U   R K U Z ,
V H Z   B O V Y R G   O I C Z   K H   L V Y Q O
Q O Z   Z A X Z D K Z I I N Z   V U   I G C I H N Z G
L Z I D B ,   I H G   K H   V R G   I P Z   Q O Z
C K P V D   V U   L V Y Q O .   —B Q I H K B R I B   K

Q G Z   Y A L Z Y Q   C E F   Q U   L Z S E J B
O U U L   J Y   Q U   D Z   E B   G U B Z Y Q   S E B .

—B E O U M Z U B   D U B E O E L Q Z

GK UCTYK JCPVKNXKV OB GFLZ

GK EKKN DLSLONK JE TJAMY,

GFANK JZFKPV UCTYK CV OB

GFLZ GK FLXK LNPKLTB TJMK.

—FKMPB GLTVGJPZF NJMYEKNNJG

PWAFFAR QIA MCA UZIJAMUVW, UZI

MCAS JAM MCA PAMMAI ADAG ZU

MCAHI PWVGRAIF.   —UIHARIHOC

BHWCAWL GHAMXFOCA

RYCLCBM GV ICC TFIR DZRL MCE

FAR FI IZR PCIICB CH MCEA

SEAVR. —TEYGEV FLLFREV VRLRYF

NJ LXSJ BFSJEOY VX DJJQ VAJ

HXXSI XE ZXOS AJFSV IAOV VAFP

VAJ HXXSI XE ZXOS AXOIJ.

—KXAFPP CXYEMFPM WXP

MXJVAJ

FRIBMQ PDYTAR KQ UBIQZ KS
NDQ QVFXEAQ YC NDQ
FMMYXEABPDQR, ZYN KS YZQ'P
YGZ XQFUQO QVEQOBQZMQ.

                          —RFUYKQON R. OTZQP

KL FTP HPJ TLL WGWSFJAKDQ
PDJKB FTP'SW NPSW TL KJ,
FTP'BB QWJ DTJAKDQ RTDW.

                          —DTSEID GKDMWDJ HWIBW

JX JI ASIQ XT OA GJPL SFV FTX
LSDCLXQ; JX JI VJRRJPDBX XT
OA HTTG SFV FTX CGDYOBA.

                              —PTFRDPJDI

XP OTN ZQQR OTNH DTNMV
WVNM OTN UXGG KQSQH RNM
OTNH PTTM XK XM.

                              —JNWMXK T'DJGGQO

17

WV WR XUVVUA VL FWJU AWDI
VIZO VL HWU AWDI.

—RZKMUF SLIORLO

18

SNR SKTR SP CSPB SZVJKOH KC
LNRO SNR PSNRG BRGCPO OPFC
NKC NRZF ZYYKGTZSKARVI QMS
CZIC OPSNKOH.

—NROGI C. NZCJKOC

19

UX UQ G EUQBHGWIB QXGXB FS
EUYV XF TGMB SBC XTUYOQ XF
VBQUHB GYV EGYJ XTUYOQ XF
SBGH.   —SHGYPUQ WGPFY

20

HUKAT XLP DLNA XLUA YT
KDWAMT, SBD DY HAD DIA TBMM
OLMBA YT CYQ, QYB VBWD ILOA
WYVASYEQ DY EKOKEA KD GKDI.

—VLUN DGLKP

Z IJJR TWAHOFOP WA FJH JFTD
UJUMTZP OYOPDEVOPO, KMH
ZXHOP Z EVWTO VO SFJEA
AJLOHVWFI.   —EWTAJF LWGFOP

ZAXZTA IATJXN ENZLXMA GPAQ
DPAW PKMA QX NXJAT OSD
DPANIATMAI DX BXZW.

                —XTEMAL VXTJINEDP

TW PJJ LPSQDJM ZOANX, QDPQ
GDNXD SLPXDLA QDL WPSQDLAQ
NKQT DLPYLK NA QDL ULPQNKH
TW P JIYNKH DLPSQ.

                —DLKSM GPSF ULLXDLS

BGFECBD WJB PKCBD OGV YMJWM
PVF FEM FKCVTYE GL YKCBWCYRMZ.

                —KJRYE IJRXG MTMKZGB

INPGLO NR YPUNROBFPGMK, VLG
MUYYNEORR NR UVFIO YPUNRO.

—UPNRGFGZO

XKW MSLJX HD NKCJV WIWP
JDYWY CY XKW DHW KW GSY
EDYX ULHCYKWV MDP.

—NWYSPW TWNNSPCS

QOS RPCYZH SCL JERP PER FOES
YFCS CLPAKR, CSZM PER
FZAORYKAR. —ROOHEO WOCS

OR JOQ QYRHUQCRG QLORHG KG
GLHQIB; OR JOQ QYRHUQCRG
OKCGRDZ KG CKBOLN. —DPQ LWX

XD HLJDVL F TRLJXFXDS DM
DWL'T DGW ICML CT XD LTJFRL
XEL TYMMLSCWB DM ICML.

                    —DTJFS GCIQL

B YXHPBWD THC HT CSW TS
YXDEFRHIHBN HC WKD LSXNR BT
B YFUNHI HCRDIDCIG.

              —QHAFDN RD IDXPBCWDT

LTIINGYEE NE EUWYUGY FU
DUQY, EUWYFLNGO FU JU, TGJ
EUWYFLNGO FU LUIY XUH.

                  —PLNGYEY IHUQYHZ

AUGUST

Answer on page 97

1

RB C PCE AMLW EMY QLLS SCJL
DRYT TRW JMPSCERMEW, SLUTCSW
RY RW KLJCZWL TL TLCUW C
ARBBLULEY AUZPPLU.
— TLEUF ACHRA YTMULCZ

2

Answer on page 98

HUBEZX MK VSZ XMK ZXBZ XBK
MZ, GPZ XMK ZXBZ UVNSRK MZ.
— GUVNBQMV DIBVYEMV

3

Answer on page 99

DLO BYVPD BIVDM MOFVP IB
UYBO BCVTYPL DLO DORD, DLO
VOQFYTYTH DLYVDM DLO
EIQQOTDFVM.
— FVDLCV PELINOTLFCOV

4

Answer on page 100

JVG FOGZJGBJ XP PZYDJB RB JX EG
IXSBIRXYB XP SXSG.
— JVXTZB IZODADG

5

Answer on page 101

UR PUG PSBHL S AGST PDYU BGIR
PDBB MRIRA PSBH YUSY AGST SBGMR
SCSDM. —FUSABRL YUGZSL TSIDL

6

Answer on page 102

YCSKS JT OF RKSBYSK GFBO YCBO
B THPVBYCSYJN SBK. —EKBOW YHRSK

7

Answer on page 103

BPSBJP IUP IJZINQ DSST VSLBIGN
ZFPG KFPN IUP TSEGD ZFIK KFPN
UPIJJN PGOSN. —QILHPJ MHKJPU

8

Answer on page 104

TJAB FBX SRDW MBVROAB SYBG
YREB AZFBSYJXP SZ ARG;
NZZDA, MBVROAB SYBG YREB SZ
ARG AZFBSYJXP. —IDRSZ

9

Answer on page 106

QM SY CPBEK OU QM EYXYPBY
QAY LCVJQU ML MQAYEU VWMP
MVEUYJXYU. —CJYTCPGYE WMWY

YPDDMKOJJ MJ P LMKO CQ WYO

BPBOJW IMKWPNO, PKT JOOAJ

MKJMDMT WC P IXSNPB WPJWO.

—SCNPK DOPBJPSS JAMWY

APXH OL DPBWR'L HVHYRWA

LSYORK WRE BWR'L HVHYRWA

MWAA. —ZHAHR YPDAWRE

SPKJ PZ G REJRGEGDPUQ KUE DIJ

KMDMEJ, GQA DIJ OJZD

REJRGEGDPUQ KUE DIJ KMDMEJ

PZ DU SPYJ GZ PK DIJEJ FJEJ

QUQJ. —JSOJED IMOOGEA

KUB ZBJXBK AC GBHMF

YHZBXLGDB HZ KA ULQB

DBHZVXB KA GAKUBX LGAVK

RUBKUBX SAV LXB ULIIS AX

MAK. —FBAXFB GBXMLXW ZULR

14

Answer on page 109

CWMIYCX YJ JW XWWK FJ YM JBBUJ
DBEWGBIFCK.   —XBWGXB BOYWM

15

Answer on page 108

YS TYF PQETM VUFG YOM FTG
QSMFVQZSM SEMOIC ZFDSM KF
EG SGP FA YOM TSEIKY.
                    —TOIIOED YERIOKK

16

Answer on page 109

IDP IBZJQUP AEID IDP AZBUG EY
IDCI IDP YIJNEG CBP LZLOYJBP
CSG IDP ESIPUUEMPSI TJUU ZT
GZJQI.   —QPBIBCSG BJYYPUU

17

Answer on page 112

HSOKO FI EW OAPQGHFWE CFXO
GAYOKIFHZ. —VOENGUFE AFIKGOCF

18

Answer on page 115

IMB MXJU XE MLVVKSBDD
PBTXWBD WXUB NBQTXWB NMBS
KI KD SXI BCVBTIBH.   —MXULTB

19

Answer on page 114

T SZVQU SZTS QALAIB WAAJD
RAX VD DNWIAY RAPQI.

—FAZTQQ ZNVQXVMZ
CNDSTWAKKV

20

Answer on page 124

NUZ ATHNZGT EJ VCJZ CH BEN P
LGERVZA NE RZ HEVSZI; CN CH P
GZPVCNT NE RZ ZWLZGCZBYZI.

—SPB IZG VZZOM

21

Answer on page 125

CF'Y D PCOB TJ YECICFKDR
YOTXXZIH FQDF SDPZY EZTERZ
FQCOP FQZH WDO XZ QDEEH
NCFQTKF STOZH. —DRXZIF WDSKY

22

Answer on page 117

TN T'G XRVER T ELQ UVTRU ZV
STHI QV SVRU, T'G JLHI ZLXIR
AIZZIK WLKI VN BOQISN.

—SIVR ISGKIG

23

Answer on page 122

OC RXBEPEUPTN PT CWLB RSUJ,
UJWLNJ CWL QWBQXPU UJX
DPUUDX, CWL NSPT UJX NBXSU.

—BSDRJ MSDAW XFXBEWT

24

Answer on page 119

SJPZP UI FWP ZPNIFW OJD OP
TNWWFS TFHAMNUW FB MUBP; US
VPPAI WF FWP NLNUWIS JUI OUMM.

—MXTUXI NWWNPXI IPWPTN

25

Answer on page 120

WT PDW SIDAAC HIZTPIN D XTTA
MWYGA JI NYTQN DNEGWV
KMINYGTWN. —ZJDSAIN NYIGWPIYU

26

Answer on page 121

UTWG CLE TDFW VL PDOW D
ITLYIW DGJ JLG'V PDOW YV,
VTDV YZ YG YVZWRK D ITLYIW.

—UYRRYDP QDPWZ

puzzles • 65

RNQGQAJJ UQG XAQAFPJNOS MPFD
OWA OFZA DPFUKNOS PM WZDUQ
UEONPQJ. —XAFDUNQA GA JOUAK

JXZS XV TZ NCD, CZ UQ NAXXZQ,
JCHQ SAPZ UXIFR QPSAQI C MCFCNQ
XI C MIPZXD. —WXAD FTEEXNH

UXRT DTRTM GQTE XP EZYMRYZQXD,
ISZ XPZTD XP QDGQATEZQXD.
—DQDXD GT UTDBUXE

XB HVCL, MPLIL XY EHFEUY VBL
FPV NXYYLY EBO VBL FPV VSSLIY
MPL TPLLN. —SILBTP GIVCLIW

BEH OSFPQJGW RSBEH EHINTQHP
WEJG NTG RQN NS SKNRQN TQB.
—BQHHE EHNFQB

September

1   *Answer on page 110*

PEXYSQ YLX SPJX KAX QKYLQ:

MX OXHXL LXYBA KAXR, GWK

SPJX KAX RYLPOXLQ IU KAX

QXY, MX BAYLK IWL BIWLQX GD

KAXR.   —BYLS QBAWLN

2   *Answer on page 98*

KNLZHGHS IGVMREV VMRESMV

GO KLJRZ KROV; VMRESMV

IGVMREV KNLZHGHS GO

YNZGKREO.   —TRHQETGEO

3   *Answer on page 99*

ICV PLLGZUC EDA ICV AVEA EGLDV

DVBVX FCEDMV ICVZX LQZDZLDU.

          —REHVU XWUUVGG GLKVGG

4   *Answer on page 100*

RD X QPXER JDECPN JDE

JESPBNFQSL XBN XJJPHRSDB, RQP

HQXECF DJ FDVSRZNP XEP KPEI

FQDER-VSKPN.   —JXBBI WZEBPI

5

Answer on page 107

WMQ BQJ GI GRP EDIQ DU GI S
CDXVEQA KSPX, VGGA SXA DEE
WGVQWMQP.

—BDEEDSC UMSNQUYQSPQ

6

Answer on page 108

ZUUF ISJJ SQ LBC UTC DTF UTJM
DQQCL LBDL AUPRCLSLSUT
ADTTUL GTFCKQCJJ UK
FCQLKUM.   —PDKQBDJJ XSCJF

7

Answer on page 103

YQ YU QSL NELXQLUQ TJ XRR
XZWXMQXNLU QT LMHTK MT
XZWXMQXNL XQ XRR.

—SLMEK ZXWYZ QSTELXV

8

Answer on page 105

OKAWHVJGL NHYOM H EOGEZO
OHMX VG ZOHK, DAV
KJQQJWAZV VG KFJPO; OHMX VG
UGPOFL, DAV JNEGMMJDZO VG
OLMZHPO.   —BOLFX DFGAUBHN

9   *Answer on page 104*

GIN FRRBX PN RSNH KHF LMRXN
NKLI FKO FNLDFN GIN MDJNX PN
MDJN.   —YMRBK PIDGGNERBN

---

10   *Answer on page 106*

IGCMM ZEJ XMMQ E WMLCMI PU
INH HU IGMZ ECM FMEF.
      —YMTOEZPT UCETXSPT

---

11   *Answer on page 101*

TVRQAV ZQW TVXKE, LQENKHVA
GVBB; JEH GFVE ZQW FJDV
LQENKHVAVH, JLS.   —NJBBWNS

---

12   *Answer on page 102*

LTRTC EXCKTB ZFQB Q SQL IQHI
BX HXO ZFTL FT UI QLKCH.
      —FTLCH ZQCM DTTJFTC

---

13   *Answer on page 109*

NC GMCE CMOYOIU VY EVYQCS,
DZN NC GMCE CMO'Y MOVXADCW
VY XOMVZY.   —SVMMF FMNWVS

14

Answer on page 97

KSEESG EW JTHSGBELTH ECS PWGNH

ECLT QWTHSVT ZE.—ALSNZQ DGWISGK

15

Answer on page 110

DBCKC'I AZ KCGCQJ XPD SLDMCATC,

RBCA SCZSEC LKC PAQZAC XJ

DBCMK ZRA WZEEJ.   —LCIZS

16

Answer on page 111

YJSZ NLD GHG NAVZATGSN

ITASZAV ZLGSN'V

IHTIDCVZSRIAV. —ZJLCSV XESRGH

17

Answer on page 112

GRFY XFZZ JUNPFQ P ZPQA MB

GRU BJUU MQZD YM ZMQL PY FG

FY GRU RMNU MB GRU HJPSU.

                    —UZNUJ APSFY

18

Answer on page 122

RAL RFCSYML OERA DCJR CQ SJ

EJ RANR OL OCSMP FNRALF YL

FSEHLP YW IFNEJL RANH JNZLP YW

KFEREKEJD.—HCFDNH ZEHKLHR ILNML

19

Answer on page 114

JUGZG XI YPJUXYD JUG HPRB
IQAAGZI JUKJ JUG IPQM FKB YPJ
WZPAXJ HB. —DGPZDG FGZGRXJU

20

Answer on page 115

JIAOEZ OH DOPZ HQUR; VTZ
HUXVZN OV XJDDH, VTZ DUQMZN
OV IRZDDH GWUQ, JQI VTZ IZZWZN
OV HOQPH OQVU, VTZ SOQI.
　　　—HJSGZD VJBDUN EUDZNOIMZ

21

Answer on page 116

R SKEQ TMJ'A R OTEQ; TU TA
UWTCM KXA GKX'WW JCHCE
DRADL TA RBRTJ.
　　　　　　—EXMMTRJ NEKHCEO

22

Answer on page 118

NFLD'Y WHDQUDYU QXTFDMDADCU
FY UTD XSCUFCKQN HD-AQPFCW
SL VSKHYDNL YS UTQU QU NQYU
VSK PCSO TSO US NFMD.
　　　　　　—OFCLHDZ HTSZDY

23

Answer on page 117

DGHGPJ TOZDBC HVO ODTHV

HVO NODXOC KVELV CGPPOT

NOJH EH.   —MOATM LVTECHAZV

                         NELVHOJIOTM

24

Answer on page 119

EAJ XMSXBEXZJ YD X VXM KJKYFP

OW EAXE YBJ JBCYPW WJSJFXT

EOKJW EAJ WXKJ ZYYM EAOBZW

DYF EAJ DOFWE EOKJ.

 —DFOJMFORA LOTAJTK BOJEIWRAJ

25

Answer on page 120

UZHB DBYZWE JW XQB JXQBO

EZMB JH MBEVPZO.

                 —TBPW-VPAU EPOXOB

26

Answer on page 121

ICLAVYCO AVIA YT MPZAV

HCPMYCO PCW SZIJAYJIUUL

AWIJVWT PCWTWUN, ICQ AVW

ZWTA PGAZEQWT YATWUN

TPPCWZ PZ UIAWZ.   —TIHY

NGRORQLXN XMN XRON

ENXBNNQ XMN RPNL LQP XMN

LIX, LQP ASFU PUNLOH BRGG

ENISON UNLGRXRNH.

—ZNLQ-ZLITFNH USFHHNLF

HI OZ NOEZ HI QSEE EZSWVTZ

SBHZEESPZBHEU SW HMZ ENWH

FTILVAH IQ ASCSESYNHSIB.

—OZTHTNBL TVWWZEE

TGDYUQDYT QU QT DGWY

QDIGWULBU UG EQTNGCYW OALU

GBY NLBBGU EG UΛLB OALU GBY

NLB EG.   —KQB SZULBF

FQYB QV KHLB EI RY VRWV,

VJQYYFBV HJL VKQFBV, ZQXM

VJQYYFBV ISBLRKQJHXQJT.

—ZQFFQHK VULJBU IRSXBS

1

Answer on page 97

VZHUH ON JP TUHCVHU NPUUPS

VZCJ VP UHQCKK C VOIH PA

ZCBBOJHNN SZHJ OJ IONHUE.

—GCJVH CKOTZOHUO

2

Answer on page 98

RU DEI XMNN XOM XCIXO DEI

VES'X OKLM XE CMWMWTMC

KSDXORSA. —WKCZ XYKRS

3

Answer on page 99

OGF RSMKMAQI OGUQLFS

WJDWNP PAPRFZOP OGWO GF

HWN YF PARFSKUZUWJ.

—YFQVWHUQ IUPSWFJU

4

Answer on page 101

YW YH LOMLTH L ZJGLW VYHWLEG

WU BUVVLQK MAGQ TUF LJG QUW

HFJG TUF MYOO XG UXGTGK.

—AUQUJG, BUVWG KG VYJLXGLF

ZGC PICQZCKZ GQDDLXCKK LK ZJ
ZIQXKWJIU JXC'K WCCOLXPK LXZJ
QVZLJX.   —PCIUQLXC SC KZQCO

F RCFXW NMBB YN AYMXFJC FPG
ARCCXNMBPCDD PCCGD F BVWWBC
GFPJCX NXYL WVLC WY WVLC, YX
WRC KYXBG JCWD MPTCFXFTBC.
                —NXVCGXVAR KVBRCBL
                       PVCWSDARC

KWZ WRCIZYK KRYX TV KWZ
JOCN'Y NOVZ OY KT ECTUZ KT R
PRA KWRK WOY OAKZAKOTAY
RCZ YZCOTGY. —WZNZA CTBNRAI

UH HQVTRHGV CNLLNRDEUNVZ
NZ UH VAMVTNVJRV UWV LDEE
CVENKWU HL VANZUVJRV.
                —YTUWDT ZRWHMVJWYDVT

FCHHSYXML XF IGS POZ DH GCUOM
ESXMLF; ZOY XF IGS POZ DH IGS
QCMLPS. —UDGOMKOF LOMKGX

R HRU HRX ATUTF, SQRF RUK TEQX
LJYATGY CTWJUV. —HRJHTUJKQO

KQDBBDG WB YD AYM DCSDHZB
EMZYWET, LMF YD BYNQQ EDPDF KD
GWBNSSMWEZDG.—NQDCNEGDF SMSD

JDXSFAXII QI AZF IZ CVTO S
TXDFSQA IQHX SI S TXDFSQA
EVSUQFB QA BZVD UQGX.
—MOQUUQMI LDZZYI

XDLCL KW WGOCGLZQ OHQ
FOWWKUH TKXDUMX WXCMBBZL.
—OZILCX GOSMW

NU OPL YFV SPNES RP IVYHV

UPPRGFNERB NE RCV BYEXB PU

RNTV, OPL'X JVRRVF QVYF QPFW

BCPVB.   —IV SFYEX FNDCYFXB

EVX ZBOQ EVNBY BXSXMMPLQ

JZL EVX ELNWRGV ZJ XUNO NM

JZL YZZI RXB EZ IZ BZEVNBY.

          —XIRWBI AWLFX

NAA OZF NPBSNAW FIUFMO SNP

JPGX OZNO OZF MHBPUBMNA

EKWBPFWW GQ ABQF BW OG

FPYGL BO.   —WNSKFΛ EKOAΓII

QXOM FSH TZQ AG QXG AGMQ ZE

SBB KZMMOABG UZWBIM, ADQ QZ

MSH QXSQ OQ OM QXG UZWMQ

OM FGWG KGQDBSTQ TZTMGTMG.

          —QXZFSM XGTWH XDYBGH

KDJFSJFZSJF KDZSI JDF ID ZQKT
OEDZ BESGF VSGCFT GI OEDZ
OSV VGJFI. —SLUKFSFQI

FYRM IQRYWUM AJ ZQF QZBH W
KWBBQQZ XQY YAJAZU KRF WBJQ
W NWYWIORFM XQY XWBBAZU.
—BRTCAU KQYZM

CXRG NI EOFG NKG JIWCV CGBB
VXYYXATCN YIW GOAK INKGW.
—ZGIWZG GCXIN

WQ IYX KWFD GY MA HYTAR,
HYTA.—HXBWXF NZZNAXF FAZABN

TP WXOFX AW THIXWKF AZF HTPO,
RF WDQZA UFBB AW UFJXP AZJP AW
NWPAFHIUJAF. —XFPF OFBNJXAFB

23

Answer on page 112

WEYYZ OX PWN CEG LWM BOGFX
LOXFMC, BMH WN XNEHRWNF EGF
BMJGF.   —XEEFOE TEMG

24

Answer on page 119

WOA OLNWIUZ IX ASAUZ EIMFWUZ
VAHLFN LF WOA OAJUW IX ASAUZ
YJF IU DIYJF.   —DLPPJ EJWOAU

25

Answer on page 114

NJXDWIGED FV WSI SGIVFJD N YNW;
FI FV CFIAFW.   —JNXFJ KENBVSW

26

Answer on page 121

FUO YDFDWO BJYCDOJVOK FUO
QWOKOJF MDKF GK ZDVU GK FUO
QGKF.   —YWBOTWBVU PBCUOCZ
                              JBOFSKVUO

27

Answer on page 125

WFJQDSOPS MT AJQSV JFDH MB
R GRF WFJQT QZRU BRNUT FJU
UJ IJUZSV RIJYU.   —VJISVU DHFO

LVHPR LVCL LVAJS AL

BRDOAPPAWYR LH LRYY EVALR

YARP PHHJ MDHE QHYHD-WYAJN.

     —CIPLAJ H'OCYYRF

FMP AVMC PIX IAT, MYN PIX'ZZ

JYIA AVMC GH PIXD IAY.

    —UTYWMQGY ODMYJZGY

IJK SCPG UW OJUFJ GTW

KLAKPUKWFKY IJK PKTEUIB CS

JUY NTEMKY UY AEKTYMPK.

     —TBW PTWX

IRJAL AJVY, YFBBWKMO IJVY,

JMC KDWKYX OBIRKMY OZTTM,

ABDIKMT FKVX FKVAXTY ZKCKMO

IZBBDY VB AXJRRTMOT

XJRRBFTTM.   —JMBM.

NOVEMBER

1 *Answer on page 97*

MGBE QPNEH AVB KU HWPNX VBE
UVHZ XP HTUVM, KYX XWUGN
UAWPUH VNU XNYRZ UBERUHH.

     —LPXWUN XUNUHV

2 *Answer on page 98*

ILB FBEE GKB LPE IG JG, ILB
FBEE IAOB GKB MAKJE IG JG AI
AK.   —FGXJ WLBEIBXMABFJ

3 *Answer on page 99*

MTVMDLMBEM LQ BRY PXKY
XKVVMBQ YR K AKB; LY LQ PXKY
K AKB FRMQ PLYX PXKY XKVVMBQ
YR XLA. —KJFRWQ XWTJMZ

4 *Answer on page 102*

RIJGJ FL UKRJT MJLL VETZJG FT
RIJ RIFTZL SJ KJEG RIET FT RIJ
RIFTZL SJ VJLFGJ.

    —PUIT AIXGRUT AUMMFTL

BLWINPNV GO VGSLI FV BVFTS
GT FYV BFVRQ GO NHWXIRZ BLWI
GO VGSLI FV BVFTS GT ILN
GTQGPGQYWR LYUWT LNWVI.

            —UWVSWVNI RNXJGN

JNP OPRJ DCZ JK FNPPI
ZKAIRPTV HR JK JIZ JK FNPPI
RKUPOKEZ PTRP.   —UCIW JDCHY

UFH RXZH NH JX, UFH RXZH NH
QDM JX; UFH RXZH KOWL NH
DZH, UFH RXZH SHAWOZH NH
FDYH.   —NASSADR FDPSAUU

RSXV YJ YEJVUW B JXVHYVJ SW
RBXXYTVJJ, BTA XVMRBXJ ERV
HRYVW RBXXYTVJJ GRYHR ERYJ
GSMUA BWWSMAJ.

            —JBPQVU OSRTJST

KMCNFKEFMC MX EAJ TFCO OMJP
CME URYUQP DVFCL
KMCNFKEFMC MX EAJ AJUVE.
—RGK OJ NUGNJCUVLGJP

WIC OTVW SGZZGM FZ FL ZI JGZ
CFLRIO ZWXU JIER, XUR ZI JGZ
TURGMLZXURFUJ ZWXU LFEYGM.
—LIEIOIU

WABFIODNB ITN FQWBN
YTCPQFYLD FQCHPB KWL BNN
UQNH KWL FIJN KWLT NKNB WYY
FQN PWID.   —QIHHIQ SWTN

FYY DEI QECLASCC LA YLVS LC
PLNB ZDLAO; SAKDHRSAN FAZ
CEVVSILAO MDRS QH NBSRCSYUSC.
—KDBFAA PDYVOFAO UDA
ODSNBS

13

Answer on page 101

JNC XSSKBKNWD NYU UWUBMUC
JO RXXC BKMKTUGD PZX CX GXM
EXMU. —RUXYRU VUNG GNMZNG

14

Answer on page 110

VMR VEXXU E XJSLMI PL FJXJIFL
NXMI ZVJ FJXZV MC VPL
OSEZPZNFJ. —BMVI QPGGJS

15

Answer on page 111

YVG LWWR YVFY NT NB QWZ NT
YVG LWWR YVFY QWZ RW UWM
WYVGMT. —MWLGM KFKTWB

16

Answer on page 106

QP FGA NRCL LVI THIJICL LG UI
KQPPIHICL PHGO LVI TRJL, JLAKF
LVI TRJL. —URHAYV JTQCGER

17

Answer on page 107

ZMYUD XMY TJWWYZ BDGDGLDB
ZMD RJUZ JBD TYWNDGWDN ZY
BDRDJZ VZ. —ODYBOD UJWZJFJWJ

18

Answer on page 104

OIPJROX XGWBP VBN WZWG
BKJRWZWY VRPJITP WOPJTNRBNE.

—GBAUJ VBAYI WEWGNIO

19

Answer on page 118

ZUHP KLQ HPDLK XLWYPM KLQB
PHYMUALB YG IHEOHO GL AH E
WYBGQH.   —JEUXYX MYABEP

20

Answer on page 115

ETZEVT DOQY IZRVG LOXS R
HTRXOXI OX VOLT.

—HRKDTVV HRVQC

21

Answer on page 119

TXRW KEBBGP SG GB JXPYGLP
NLKY RGASWPPXBS.

—YGBGAW UW HETMEK

22

Answer on page 117

QZBBZH HUEFU EQ TSXSB
QVZNST EQ IUS USGXESQI MZGO
IZ CSGB.   —QGDKSM CKIMSB

23

Answer on page 114

AI AR TMN IJAMX IT BVCARN

GARPABWAMN, CMG CMTIJNV IT

RSFKAI IT AI.

—KAXSNW GN PNVLCMINR

24

Answer on page 116

LAX LTBYEP DUJ WDF GXU LTJ

TJDUL: UIYYBYE IR PLDBUP DYF

UIYYBYE FXAY RJXROJ.

—WJUYDUF WDUIHT

25

Answer on page 108

KWOOSKK YK R UVYKVP ACRA

KCVWFX VPFM LS ARZSP FRAS YP

FYDS, RPX ACSP VPFM YP KJRFF

XVKSK.   —RPACVPM ABVFFVUS

26

Answer on page 121

QGC IKUH XQQTXOQCH DJ NGXQ

KV AXWVC GXV UY TCWKVG AYT

DCQQCT QGKUSV.   —GYTXOC

27

Answer on page 122

YZM DPNJOBE QKP
MUGMPOMBDM OI YZM
CMEOBBOBE KQ OWWHIOKB.

—LOVVH TPOIZBNRHPYO

28

Answer on page 123

BIQ VMDQVB TFR EZB BZ NFGS
GV BZ JQBQDAGEQ BZ VMXXQQJ.

—DGXIFDJ PDGEVSQR VIQDGJFE

29

Answer on page 120

CQS'W OMOI LPRK R CQQI; FQJ
KGNTW ZRSW WQ NQ DRBU.

—CQS TOIQPC

30

Answer on page 125

RXBBVRRJXT RΓCVLR FLV
RMLFGHAM-MAGYEGYH
RZVYKVLR. —AFLCVD F. NTPKHVMM

DECEMBER

1   Answer on page 97

IFP QJK VFC HJK IFJKR FWQXPSA
JSCKP ACL IFP FJZZWKPXX FP
PKTCMX WX ILBSM ESPXXPN.

—CSWDPL UCSNXQWIF

2   Answer on page 98

BADF VT E KAAX MYFEHQETP,
MNP VP VT E MEX TNDDFY.

—QYEWZVT MEZAW

3   Answer on page 99

ULZPADMQ TC HYD LD LUU L GLI
GMPTHHTHP OYQ L OQTMHICATN,
LHI TD TC OLQ DAM GMCD
MHITHP OYQ YHM. —YCJLQ STUIM

4   Answer on page 100

Z GJHO GPXT RZC HJW DT OJJA
THJQOK, DQW Z OJJA GPXT PI
GJHO THJQOK.

—DTHUZRPH XEZHMGPH

5

Answer on page 105

KDS DZQRX HRFS VL VX KDS
PSLK FIXTVKVIX ODSX VK DRL
KDS NHSRKSLK TSNHSS IE
GVPSHKB.— TRXKS RGVNDVSHV

6

Answer on page 102

SJ KDSH FNIWX SK SH JNK FDLK
FC KLAC ZE, YZK FDLK FC TSUC
ZE, KDLK VLACH ZH ISMD.

—DCJIQ FLIX YCCMDCI

7

Answer on page 103

XH LGX TGX TAMLF HDI FJPHXY
ICJ AMLMIGIMHX HO CMW HVX
TCGBGTIJB.   —ZHCX LHBAJP

8

Answer on page 104

JNJR LEJ EJMNJRC MFJ RAL
DZZBGDRMLJQ HV KBCL ARJ
CLMF; CA, LAA, GMR'C UARQBUL
UMRRAL HJ HMCJQ AR KBCL ARJ
GALDNJ.   —CMMQDM OMAR

9

Answer on page 101

TNRROKHWW UNFHW PR OK
THOJTY ATNY OY DNEFW OK
DHKJYT.   —QXGHQY IQXWY

10

Answer on page 106

DR CPZZNKG IS ZAN ANPKZ,
RIZADRO DG ZKBN NFLNMZ ZAN
DCMKIHPHUN.

          —ONKCPDRN QN GZPNU

11

Answer on page 107

NMZ XSZ BZGTXAB YXSJTYNTXS
NMON O QOS BMXAIH MOJZ TB
NMON SXNMTSL TB NX PZ NOVZS
NXX BZGTXABIW.—BOQAZI PANIZG

12

Answer on page 108

JNIQ NT ZAA TKAVZ, HOY ZKQ
ZNPQ RQ RHTZQ NO BHRONOM
OQEQV UHO FQ VQMHNOQY.

          —TZQOYKHJ

13

Answer on page 109

I FIE AWT KYIUH AJXWTPX HWIFC
AJMM RJEL UYCIX LJRRJSPMXN
JE MJZJEU PD XT WJH KYIUUJEU.

—STERPSJPH

14

Answer on page 110

AGBAKJEYZIYGZN HPGUHIAH GE
NGXH Z DNZAXDHBBV, SMGAM
SMHI BHU TB SMGYH GE BHZNNV
LBHHI.   —ZKEYGI T'JZNNHV

15

Answer on page 114

LAD TJGNALDXL TWKYDX BQ
NWKHODXX KJD ZBEEBOWF
MGOHWDH TF VODRUDZLDH
XUKJMX.   —XKEVDW IBAOXBO

16

Answer on page 115

VW AMTZE EM CMGETZW HI
UWJWGSF UEWDU, HTE GWPTQGW
MZFI MZW EM YMAW BMVZ.

—UESZQUFSU Q

DBSCAQ BY BG ESQWC PWGEQS
HFQG BC MQEBGY CT MSBGE
ETTP SQYAUCY.　—RTFG MQSSO

QPA XH AXBA BWPOQM CEA XH
AXBA BWPOHM KBZHM B
WJSJQJAL.　—CBUABMBO NOBFJBQ

IPESZNXR RJKBNL HXPXNC RJKI
IJXPX GJX RHENXR JDYX WXXS.
　　　　　　　—HDPZ GIDES

IBPD DNDSF XHHW CABYX BY
IBTD, E XEBY BYNHINDU E
UEKSBTBKD. —KAESIDU H'KHYYDII

ALX AWKTXVXW HUALZDA
ZECXWTKAUZF UC K EUWO
HUALZDA HUFRC.　—CKKOU RKZF

22

Answer on page 117

ALQ YJQFAQCA AJHALC FJQ ALQ
CDRZVQCA, FMU CP FJQ ALQ
YJQFAQCA RQM.   —F. I. LFJQ

23

Answer on page 118

FNA JSKG FNSF OSMA XG NSCCK
OSMA XG EVGA.—HZNR OSGAPVAWJ

24

Answer on page 119

XJXEOK LUX EXJXU LHKQDVOX,
LEG OZXCU QVOAQFX GXIXEGK
XEOCUXDP VIQE OZX CEGCJCGVLD.
               —ZQEQUX GX HLDWLA

25

Answer on page 120

ZXRJTX ZUBHA MLG AHMARLA
HQHI FXMLIH, MLG VIUHLGA
TIRN AFMIFH MLG VHN, BMP
HMFX AJFFHHGULT FXIUAZBMA
DIULT VIHAX XRKHA MLG CRPA
ZR PRJ.   —BMLAHSS

MIMBA NOR FOJ O BKTFV VQ FKJ

QGKRKQR, CZV RQ NOR FOJ O

BKTFV VQ CM EBQRT KR FKJ

YODVJ.   —CMBROBH COBZDF

LOH RXLXJH OFI F OFKDL CR

IXGGHQET FQG GJFNFLDMFEET

KHMCNDQB LOH WJHIHQL.

          —JCBHJ KFKICQ

FHA SZHHFV EA AHQKFBO ZHR

PZCCX ZV VPA OZDA VKDA.

          —PAHYX JYAEAY

XBI HIEUAD XBI LEN AO XBI

XHEDUZHIUUAH TU BEHM TU

WIKEYUI TX'U UA KHALMIM.

          —VTD BYWWEHM

OWJX WA I AMHHXAAWKU KJ

OXAAKUA DGWHG TMAV NX

OWYXL VK NX MULXPAVKKL.

—PIOEG DIOLK XTXPAKU

GMK QEY OQKJ QIG, CIG GMK

OERY BQIXO BKRW NQSKJ

SKWWAEB AX GQSQWWQV. MRZZB

XKV BKRW!

—KSAEB MIXGAXOYQX SAEEKW

Answers

January 1

May the spirit of the season gladden your heart and nourish your soul.

—Louise B. Moll

February 1

Home is not where you live but where they understand you.

—Christian Morgenstern

March 1

Humor brings insight and tolerance; irony a deeper and less friendly understanding.

—Agnes Repplier

April 1

Of all men's miseries the bitterest is to know so much and to have control over nothing.

—Herodotus

May 1

One's real life is so often the life that one does not lead. *—Oscar Wilde*

June 1

Heroism consists of hanging on one minute longer.

—Norwegian proverb

July 1

If we seek the pleasure of love, passion should be occasional, and common sense continual.

—Robertson Davies

August 1

If a man does not keep pace with his companions, perhaps it is because he hears a different drummer.

—Henry David Thoreau

September 14

Better to understand the world than condemn it.

—Gaelic proverb

October 1

There is no greater sorrow than to recall a time of happiness when in misery.

—Dante Alighieri

November 1

Kind words can be short and easy to speak, but their echoes are truly endless.

—Mother Teresa

December 1

The man who can thank himself alone for the happiness he enjoys is truly blessed.

—Oliver Goldsmith

January 2

The unfortunate thing about this world is that good habits are so much easier to give up than bad ones. *—W. Somerset Maugham*

February 2

Life is the art of drawing sufficient conclusions from insufficient premises. *—Samuel Butler*

March 2

To be content with little is hard, to be content with much impossible. *—Marie von Ebner Eschenbach*

April 2

Blessed are they who have nothing to say, and who cannot be persuaded to say it. *—James Russell Lowell*

May 2

The fate of love is that it always seems too little or too much. *—Amelia Barr*

June 2

Wherever the art of medicine is loved, there also is love of humanity. *—Hippocrates*

July 2

He that always gives way to others will end in having no principles of his own. *—Aesop*

August 2

Wealth is not his that has it, but his that enjoys it. *—Benjamin Franklin*

September 2

Learning without thought is labor lost; thought without learning is perilous. *—Confucius*

October 2

If you tell the truth you don't have to remember anything. *—Mark Twain*

November 2

The less one has to do, the less time one finds to do it in. *—Lord Chesterfield*

December 2

Hope is a good breakfast, but it is a bad supper. *—Francis Bacon*

January 3

Humanity is fortunate because no man is unhappy except by his own fault. *—Lucius Annaeus Seneca*

February 3

When our hearts are empty, we collect things.   *–Jiddhu Krishnamurti*

March 3

He is educated who knows where to find out what he doesn't know.
–Georg Simmel

April 3

The great secret of life is never to be in the way of others.
–Thomas Chandler Haliburton

May 7

The day wasted on others is not wasted on oneself.   *–Charles Dickens*

June 3

There are two days about which nobody should ever worry, and these are yesterday and tomorrow.   *–Robert Jones Burdette*

July 3

He that wants money, means, and content is without three good friends.   *–William Shakespeare*

August 3

The first forty years of life furnish the text, the remaining thirty the commentary.   *–Arthur Schopenhauer*

September 3

The foolish and the dead alone never change their opinions.
–James Russell Lowell

October 3

The profound thinker always suspects that he may be superficial.
–Benjamin Disraeli

November 3

Experience is not what happens to a man; it is what a man does with what happens to him.   *–Aldous Huxley*

December 3

Laughter is not at all a bad beginning for a friendship, and it is far the best ending for one.   *–Oscar Wilde*

January 6

Life, like every other blessing, derives its value from its use alone.
–Samuel Johnson

February 28

Conscience is a mother-in-law whose visit never ends.
–H. L. Mencken

March 4

Our most important thoughts are those which contradict our emotions. *—Paul Valéry*

April 5

To every thing there is a season, and a time to every purpose under the heaven. *—Ecclesiastes*

May 9

Happiness is a mystery, like religion, and should never be rationalized. *—G. K. Chesterton*

June 4

The best time to do a thing is when it can be done. *—William Pickens*

July 4

Every society honors its live conformists and its dead troublemakers. *—Mignon McLaughlin*

August 4

The greatest of faults is to be conscious of none. *—Thomas Carlyle*

September 4

To a heart formed for friendship and affection, the charms of solitude are very short-lived. *—Fanny Burney*

October 5

The greatest happiness is to transform one's feelings into action. *—Germaine de Staël*

November 6

The best way to cheer yourself is to try to cheer somebody else. *—Mark Twain*

December 4

A long life may not be good enough, but a good life is long enough. *—Benjamin Franklin*

January 5

It is the province of knowledge to speak, and it is the privilege of wisdom to listen. *—Oliver Wendell Holmes*

February 5

It is folly to endeavor to make ourselves shine before we are luminous. *—Horace Bushnell*

March 5

The smallest feelings are worth more than the most beautiful thoughts. *—Bernard de Fontenelle*

April 4

Faith opens a way for the understanding; unbelief closes it.

—St. Augustine

May 10

Great thoughts reduced to practice become great acts.

—William Hazlitt

June 5

Every man should keep a fair-sized cemetery in which to bury the faults of his friends. *—Henry Ward Beecher*

July 5

Consider the postage stamp: its usefulness consists in the ability to stick to one thing till it gets there. *—Josh Billings*

August 5

He who walks a road with love will never walk that road alone again. *—Charles Thomas Davis*

September 11

Before you begin, consider well; and when you have considered, act. *—Sallust*

October 4

It is always a great mistake to command when you are not sure you will be obeyed. *—Honoré, Comte de Mirabeau*

November 13

Bad officials are elected by good citizens who do not vote.

—George Jean Nathan

December 9

Happiness makes up in height what it lacks in length. *—Robert Frost*

January 4

Learn to laugh with others, and most important, at yourself.

—Frank Tyger

February 6

The best way to convince a fool that he is wrong is to let him have his own way. *—Josh Billings*

March 6

There is a time to wink as well as to see. *—Thomas Fuller*

April 13

He that loses his conscience has nothing left that is worth keeping.

—Izaak Walton

May 13

The perpetual obstacle to human advancement is custom.

—John Stuart Mill

June 6

He who has but one enemy shall meet him everywhere.

—Omar Khayyam

July 6

One of the greatest sources of suffering is to have an inborn sense of honor. *—B. Decasseres*

August 6

There is no greater loan than a sympathetic ear. *—Frank Tyger*

September 12

Never forget what a man says to you when he is angry.

—Henry Ward Beecher

October 6

A heart full of courage and cheerfulness needs a little danger from time to time, or the world gets unbearable.

—Friedrich Wilhelm Nietzsche

November 4

There is often less danger in the things we fear than in the things we desire. *—John Churton Collins*

December 6

In this world it is not what we take up, but what we give up, that makes us rich. *—Henry Ward Beecher*

January 7

No one knows what it is that he can do until he tries. *—Publius Syrus*

February 29

Music washes away from the soul the dust of everyday life.

—Berthold Auerbach

March 7

A kind heart is a fountain of gladness, making everything in its vicinity freshen into smiles. *—Washington Irving*

April 7

The human heart is like heaven; the more angels the more room.

—Fredrika Bremer

May 3

The inability to stay quiet is one of the most conspicuous failings of mankind. *—Walter Bagehot*

June 9

It is the false shame of fools which tries to cover unhealed sores.

—Horace

July 7

To make good use of life, one should have in youth the experience of advanced years, and in old age the vigor of youth.   *—Stanislas I*

August 7

People are always good company when they are doing what they really enjoy.   *—Samuel Butler*

September 7

It is the greatest of all advantages to enjoy no advantage at all.

—Henry David Thoreau

October 7

The hardest task of the girl's life is to prove to a man that his intentions are serious.   *—Helen Rowland*

November 7

The more we do, the more we can do; the more busy we are, the more leisure we have.   *—William Hazlitt*

December 7

No man can climb out beyond the limitation of his own character.

—John Morley

January 10

A tart temper never mellows with age, and a sharp tongue is the only edged tool that grows keener with constant use.

—Washington Irving

February 8

The eye is the window of the soul; the intellect and will are seen in it.   *—Hiram Powers*

March 8

If you don't know where you're going, any path will take you there.

—Sioux proverb

April 10

Nothing is so dangerous as an ignorant friend; a wise enemy is better.   *—Jean de la Fontaine*

May 8

There is nothing so nice as doing good by stealth and being found out by accident.   *—Charles Lamb*

June 8

The life of an adventurer is the practice of the art of the impossible.
—William Bolitho

July 9

We judge ourselves by what we feel capable of doing, while others judge us by what we have already done.
—Henry Wadsworth Longfellow

August 8

Wise men talk because they have something to say; fools, because they have to say something.
—Plato

September 9

The doors we open and close each day decide the lives we live.
—Flora Whittemore

October 8

To overcome difficulties is to experience the full delight of existence.
—Arthur Schopenhauer

November 18

Nothing great was ever achieved without enthusiasm.
—Ralph Waldo Emerson

December 8

Even the heavens are not illuminated by just one star; so, too, man's conduct cannot be based on just one motive.
—Saadia Gaon

January 9

Happiness is not the station we arrive at but the manner by which we arrive.
—Oliver G. Wilson

February 16

Love is the wisdom of the fool and the folly of the wise.
—Samuel Johnson

March 9

Experience is not what happens to you; it is what you do with what happens to you.
—Aldous Huxley

April 9

Everything comes to him who hustles while he waits.
—Thomas Alva Edison

May 4

Everyone complains of his memory, and no one complains of his judgment.
—François de la Rochefoucauld

June 7

There is nobody so irritating as somebody with less intelligence and more sense than we have.   *–Don Herold*

July 8

The surest way to remain poor is to be an honest man.
    –Napoleon Bonaparte

August 10

Happiness is a wine of the rarest vintage, and seems insipid to a vulgar taste.   *–Logan Pearsall Smith*

September 8

Education makes a people easy to lead, but difficult to drive; easy to govern, but impossible to enslave.   *–Henry Brougham*

October 9

Suffering is the law of human beings; war is the law of the jungle.
    –Mohandas Gandhi

November 9

Conviction of the mind does not always bring conviction of the heart.   *–Luc de Vauvenargues*

December 5

The human race is in the best condition when it has the greatest degree of liberty.   *– Dante Alighieri*

January 8

We are all travelers in the desert of life and the best we can find in our journey is an honest friend.   *–Robert Louis Stevenson*

February 17

A really busy person never knows how much he weighs.
    –Edgar Watson Howe

March 10

The deepest principle of human nature is the craving to be appreciated.   *–William James*

April 8

It is much safer to obey than to rule.   *–Thomas à Kempis*

May 5

The little knowledge that acts is worth infinitely more than much knowledge that is idle.   *–Kahlil Gibran*

June 10

It is a funny thing about life; if you refuse to accept anything but the best you very often get it.   *–W. Somerset Maugham*

July 10

Blessed are the forgetful, for they get the better even of their blunders. *—Friedrich Wilhelm Nietzsche*

August 9

To be angry is to revenge the faults of others upon ourselves.
—Alexander Pope

September 10

Three may keep a secret if two of them are dead. *—Benjamin Franklin*

October 10

A man may honor, fear and obey without loving. *—Maimonides*

November 16

If you want the present to be different from the past, study the past.
—Baruch Spinoza

December 10

In matters of the heart, nothing is true except the improbable.
—Germaine de Staël

January 11

Success does not consist in never making blunders, but in never making the same one the second time. *—Henry Wheeler Shaw*

February 23

The great pleasure in life is doing what people say you cannot do.
—Walter Bagehot

March 11

An acquaintance that begins with a compliment is sure to develop into a real friendship. *—Oscar Wilde*

April 11

There is in human nature generally more of the fool than of the wise. *—Francis Bacon*

May 17

Old age to the unlearned is winter; to the learned it is harvest time.
—Judah Leib Lazerov

June 15

Years wrinkle the skin, but to give up enthusiasm wrinkles the soul.
—Samuel Ullman

July 11

Economy is too late when you are at the bottom of your purse.
—Lucius Annaeus Seneca

August 11

Love is woman's eternal spring and man's eternal fall.

—Helen Rowland

September 5

The web of our life is of a mingled yarn, good and ill together.

—William Shakespeare

October 11

Blessed is he who expects nothing, for he shall never be disappointed.   *—Alexander Pope*

November 17

Those who cannot remember the past are condemned to repeat it.

—George Santayana

December 11

The one serious conviction that a man should have is that nothing is to be taken too seriously.   *—Samuel Butler*

January 16

Believe that life is worth living and your belief will help create the fact.   *—William James*

February 12

The best thing about the future is that it comes only one day at a time.   *—Abraham Lincoln*

March 13

Opinions cannot survive if one has no chance to fight for them.

—Thomas Mann

April 16

It is music's lofty mission to shed light on the depths of the human heart.   *—Robert Schumann*

May 12

The foolish man seeks happiness in the distance; the wise grows it under his feet.   *—James Oppenheim*

June 12

Think of all the beauty that's still left in and around you and be happy.   *—Anne Frank*

July 12

Be more careful to keep the doors of your heart shut than the doors of your house.   *—Johann Wolfgang von Goethe*

August 15

He who draws upon his own resources easily comes to an end of his wealth. — *William Hazlitt*

September 6

Good will is the one and only asset that competition cannot undersell or destroy. — *Marshall Field*

October 12

Greatness is not so much a certain size as a certain quality in your life. — *Phillips Brooks*

November 25

Success is a poison that should only be taken late in life, and then only in small doses. — *Anthony Trollope*

December 12

Life is too short, and the time we waste in yawning never can be regained. — *Stendhal*

January 13

Those who contemplate the beauty of the earth find reserves of strength that will endure as long as life lasts. — *Rachel Carson*

February 13

If you want to see what children can do, you must stop giving them things. — *Norman Douglas*

March 12

Wisdom consists in being able to distinguish among dangers and make a choice of the least harmful. — *Niccolò Machiavelli*

April 6

A homemade friend wears longer than one you buy in the market. — *Austin O'Malley*

May 6

Learning is an ornament in prosperity, a refuge in adversity, and a provision in old age. — *Aristotle*

June 13

The most important ingredient of the future is the present. — *George Leonard*

July 13

Advice should be given by the example of the accomplished, not by one's own meager experience. — *Dagobert D. Runes*

August 16
The trouble with the world is that the stupid are cocksure and the intelligent full of doubt. —*Bertrand Russell*

September 13
To know oneself is wisdom, but to know one's neighbor is genius. —*Minna Antrim*

October 13
There is scarcely any passion without struggle. —*Albert Camus*

November 5
Whatever is right or wrong in our world is exactly what is right or wrong in the individual human heart. —*Margaret Leckie*

December 13
A man who brags without shame will find great difficulty in living up to his bragging. —*Confucius*

January 14
He is not only idle who does nothing, but he is idle who might be better employed. —*Socrates*

February 14
Love sought is good, but given unsought is better. —*William Shakespeare*

March 14
Gratitude is the fairest blossom which springs from the soul. —*Henry Ward Beecher*

April 14
Let us all be happy and live within our means, even if we have to borrow the money to do it with. —*Artemus Ward*

May 18
The only genuine romance for grown people is reality. —*Thomas Carlyle*

June 14
There is nothing that costs less than civility. —*Don Quixote*

July 14
If you put off everything until you're sure of it, you'll get nothing done. —*Norman Vincent Peale*

August 14
Nothing is so good as it seems beforehand. —*George Eliot*

September 1
Ideals are like the stars: we never reach them, but like the mariners of the sea, we chart our course by them.   *—Carl Schurz*

October 14
If you are going to leave footprints in the sands of time, you'd better wear work shoes.   *—Le Grand Richards*

November 14
How happy a person is depends upon the depth of his gratitude.
—John Miller

December 14
Circumstantial evidence is like a blackberry, which when red or white is really green.   *—Austin O'Malley*

January 15
We must use time creatively and forever realize that the time is always ripe to do right.   *—Martin Luther King, Jr.*

February 15
Men their rights and nothing more; women their rights and nothing less.   *—Susan B. Anthony*

March 15
Most people put off till tomorrow that which they should have done yesterday.   *—Edgar Watson Howe*

April 15
April is the month when the green returns to the lawn, the trees and the Internal Revenue Service.   *—Evan Esar*

May 23
The ornament of a house is the friends who frequent it.
—Ralph Waldo Emerson

June 11
To establish oneself in the world, one does all one can to seem established there already.   *—François de la Rochefoucauld*

July 17
It is better to live rich than to die rich.   *—Samuel Johnson*

August 12
Life is a preparation for the future, and the best preparation for the future is to live as if there were none.   *—Elbert Hubbard*

September 15
There's no remedy but patience, when people are undone by their own folly.   *—Aesop*

October 15

The only thing necessary for the triumph of evil is for good men to do nothing.
—*Edmund Burke*

November 15

The good that is in you is the good that you do for others.
—*Roger Babson*

December 18

Not he that adorns but he that adores makes a divinity.
—*Baltasar Gracian*

January 12

It is dangerous to be sincere unless you are also stupid.
—*George Bernard Shaw*

February 9

A man who has never been in danger cannot answer for his courage.
—*François de la Rochefoucauld*

March 19

It is only people of small moral stature who have to stand on their dignity.
—*Arnold Bennett*

April 12

What is moral is what you feel good after, and what is immoral is what you feel bad after.
—*Ernest Hemingway*

May 28

Happy is he who has succeeded in learning the causes of things.
—*Virgil*

June 20

When it is a question of money, everybody is of the same religion.
—*Voltaire*

July 16

If you keep your mouth shut you will never put your foot in it.
—*Austin O'Malley*

August 13

The secret of being miserable is to have leisure to bother about whether you are happy or not.
—*George Bernard Shaw*

September 16

What you did yesterday creates today's circumstances.
—*Thomas Blandi*

October 16
All the animals except man know that the principal business of life is to enjoy it. —*Samuel Butler*

November 10
How much better it is to get wisdom than gold, and to get understanding than silver. —*Solomon*

December 19
Wrinkles should merely show where the smiles have been.
—*Mark Twain*

January 17
The right word may be effective, but no word was ever as effective as a rightly timed pause. —*Mark Twain*

February 10
It is through the cracks in our brains that ecstasy creeps in.
—*Logan Pearsall Smith*

March 17
Irish blunders are never blunders of the heart. —*Maria Edgeworth*

April 27
We don't grow older, we grow riper. —*Pablo Picasso*

May 11
The world stands or falls with the laws of life which heaven has written in the human conscience. —*Pierre van Paassen*

June 21
Most of the shadows of this life are caused by standing in our own sunshine. —*Ralph Waldo Emerson*

July 15
It is easy to be rich and not haughty; it is difficult to be poor and not grumble. —*Confucius*

August 17
There is no education like adversity. —*Benjamin Disraeli*

September 17
This will remain a land of the free only so long as it is the home of the brave. —*Elmer Davis*

October 23
Happy is the man who finds wisdom, for he searched and found.
—*Saadia Gaon*

November 11

Obstacles are those frightful things you see when you take your eyes off the goal. *—Hannah More*

December 17

Virtue is in great danger when it begins to bring good results.

—John Berry

January 18

A man who prides himself on his ancestry is like the potato plant, the best part of which is underground. *—Spanish proverb*

February 7

Our main business is not to see what lies dimly at a distance, but to do what lies clearly at hand. *—Thomas Carlyle*

March 18

Business and life are like a bank account. You can't take out more than you put in. *—William Feather*

April 18

Men's natures are alike; it is their habits that carry them far apart.

—Confucius

May 14

A person is really alive only when he is moving forward to something more. *—Winfred Rhodes*

June 18

The middle of the road is where the white line is, and that's the worst place to drive. *—Robert Frost*

July 27

Man should not wish his pain upon others, only his pleasures.

—Suudiu Guvn

August 29

Love never dies of starvation, but often of indigestion.

—Ninon de Lenclos

September 27

Eliminate the time between the idea and the act, and your dreams will become realities. *—Jean-Jacques Rousseau*

October 18

Contentment comes not so much from great wealth as from few wants. *—Epictetus*

November 8

Hope is itself a species of happiness, and perhaps the chief happiness which this world affords. —*Samuel Johnson*

December 15

The brightest blazes of gladness are commonly kindled by unexpected sparks. —*Samuel Johnson*

January 19

Every custom was once an eccentricity; every idea was once an absurdity. —*Holbrook Jackson*

February 11

Error of opinion may be tolerated when reason is left free to combat it. —*Thomas Jefferson*

March 21

The poor man is happy; he expects no change for the worse.

—*Demetrius*

April 19

Tell me what company you keep, and I'll tell you what you are.

—*Miguel de Cervantes*

May 19

In the battle for existence, talent is the punch, and tact is the clever foot work. —*Wilson Mizner*

June 29

What we see depends mainly on what we look for. —*John Lubbock*

July 19

It is a miserable state of mind to have few things to desire and many things to fear. —*Francis Bacon*

August 19

A thing that nobody looks for is seldom found.

—*Johann Heinrich Pestalozzi*

September 19

There is nothing the body suffers that the soul may not profit by.

—*George Meredith*

October 25

Adventure is not outside a man; it is within. —*David Grayson*

November 23

It is one thing to praise discipline, and another to submit to it.

—*Miguel de Cervantes*

December 16
We mount to fortune by several steps, but require only one to come down.   *—Stanislas I*

January 24
Advice is a drug in the market; the supply always exceeds the demand.   *—Josh Billings*

February 24
Dreams surely are for the spirit what sleep is for the body.
—Friedrich Hebbel

March 16
When an oak tree is felled, the whole forest echoes with it, but a hundred acorns are planted silently by some unseen force.
—Thomas Carlyle

April 20
When fortune comes, seize her in the front with a sure hand, because behind she is bald.   *—Leonardo da Vinci*

May 20
There are, in every age, new errors to be rectified, and new prejudices to be opposed.   *—Samuel Johnson*

June 16
It matters not how small the beginning may seem to be; what is once well done is done forever.   *—Henry David Thoreau*

July 24
Nothing can bring you peace but the triumph of principles.
—Ralph Waldo Emerson

August 18
The hour of happiness becomes more welcome when it is not expected.   *—Horace*

September 20
Advice is like snow; the softer it falls, the longer it dwells upon, and the deeper it sinks into, the mind.   *—Samuel Taylor Coleridge*

October 20
Live to make the world less difficult for each other.   *—George Eliot*

November 20
People with goals find a meaning in life.   *—Maxwell Maltz*

December 20
Like every good thing in life, a gain involves a sacrifice.
—Charles O'Connell

January 31

Happiness is good for the body, but sorrow strengthens the spirit.

—*Marcel Proust*

February 25

The reward of a thing well done is to have done it.

—*Ralph Waldo Emerson*

March 20

Confessions may be good for the soul but they are bad for the reputation.

—*Lord Dewar*

April 21

Grab a chance and you won't be sorry for a might-have-been.

—*Arthur Ransome*

May 21

Age does not make us childish, as people say; it only finds us still true children.

—*Johann Wolfgang von Goethe*

June 17

Life is a flower of which love is the honey.

—*Victor Hugo*

July 28

He who overcomes others is strong; he who overcomes himself is mighty.

—*Lao Tzu*

August 31

Man forgives woman anything save the wit to outwit him.

—*Minna Antrim*

September 21

A word isn't a bird; if it flies out you'll never catch it again.

—*Russian proverb*

October 21

If you wish to be loved, love.

—*Lucius Annaeus Seneca*

November 24

Two things are bad for the heart: running up stairs and running down people.

—*Bernard Baruch*

December 21

The traveler without observation is a bird without wings.

—*Saadi Gaon*

January 22

There is always one moment in childhood when the door opens and lets the future in.

—*Graham Greene*

February 22
I hold the maxim no less applicable to public than to private affairs, that honesty is always the best policy.   *—George Washington*

March 22
Even a fish wouldn't get into trouble if it kept its mouth shut.
—Korean proverb

April 25
Genius does what it must, and talent does what it can.
—Owen Meredith

May 22
Conversation enriches the understanding, but solitude is the school of genius.   *—Edward Gibbon*

June 26
When unhappy, one doubts everything; when happy one doubts nothing.   *—Joseph Roux*

July 22
People seldom improve when they have no model but themselves to copy.   *—Oliver Goldsmith*

August 22
If I'd known I was going to live so long, I'd have taken better care of myself.   *—Leon Eldred*

September 23
Autumn repays the earth the leaves which summer lent it.
—Georg Christoph Lichtenberg

October 22
In order to improve the mind, we ought less to learn than to con-template   *—René Descartes*

November 22
Sorrow which is never spoken is the heaviest load to bear.
—Samuel Butler

December 22
The greatest truths are the simplest, and so are the greatest men.
—A. W. Hare

January 23
If you do not tell the truth about yourself, you cannot tell it about other people.   *—Virginia Woolf*

February 19

No one can build his security upon the nobleness of another person.
—Willa Cather

March 23

The two greatest stimulants in the world are youth and debt.
—Benjamin Disraeli

April 23

Childhood shows the man as morning shows the day.   *—John Milton*

May 15

That help is doubly acceptable which you offer spontaneously when we stand in need.   *—Publius Syrus*

June 27

It is never too late to be what you might have been.   *—George Eliot*

July 26

The fault no child ever loses is the one he was most punished for.
—Cesare Beccaria

August 27

Kindness and generosity form the true morality of human actions.
—Germaine de Staël

September 22

Life's greatest achievement is the continual re-making of yourself so that at last you know how to live.   *—Winfred Rhodes*

October 17

This may not be the best of all possible worlds, but to say that it is the worst is mere petulant nonsense.   *—Thomas Henry Huxley*

November 19

When you enjoy loving your neighbor it ceases to be a virtue.
—Kahlil Gibran

December 23

The days that make us happy make us wise.   *—John Masefield*

January 20

There is nothing we receive with so much reluctance as advice.
—Joseph Addison

February 20

There is but one substitute for imagination, and that is experience.
—Gelette Burgess

March 24
Friendship consists in forgetting what one gives, and remembering what one receives. —*Alexandre Dumas (Père)*

April 24
Better be unborn than untaught, for ignorance is the root of misfortune. —*Plato*

May 24
A youth without fire is followed by an old age without experience.
—*Charles Caleb Colton*

June 24
Love knows no limit to its endurance, no end to its trust, no fading of its hope; it can outlast anything. —*St. Paul*

July 20
Grief can take care of itself, but to get the full value of joy, you must have somebody to divide it with. —*Mark Twain*

August 24
There is one reason why we cannot complain of life; it keeps no one against his will. —*Lucius Annaeus Seneca*

September 24
The advantage of a bad memory is that one enjoys several times the same good things for the first time. —*Friedrich Wilhelm Nietzsche*

October 24
The history of every country begins in the heart of every man or woman. —*Willa Cather*

November 21
Life cannot go on without much forgetting. —*Honoré de Balzac*

December 24
Events are never absolute, and their outcome depends entirely upon the individual. —*Honoré de Balzac*

January 25
It is easier to fight for one's principles than to live up to them.
—*Alfred Adler*

February 21
One can never consent to creep when one feels an impulse to soar.
—*Helen Keller*

March 25
The world is full of willing people; some willing to work, the rest willing to let them. —*Robert Frost*

April 22

Life is too short to be little.   —*Benjamin Disraeli*

May 31

No living being is held by anything so strongly as its own needs.
                                                   —*Epictetus*

June 25

The hardest thing to learn in life is which bridge to cross and which
to burn.   —*David Russell*

July 25

Virtue is praiseworthy, but happiness is above praise.   —*Aristotle*

August 25

No man really becomes a fool until he stops asking questions.
                                                   —*Charles Steinmetz*

September 25

Life begins on the other side of despair.   —*Jean-Paul Sartre*

October 19

True courage is not only a balloon for rising but also a parachute for
falling.   —*Ludwig Borne*

November 29

Don't ever slam a door; you might want to go back.   —*Don Herold*

December 25

Though times and seasons ever change, and friends grow scarce
and few, may each succeeding Christmas bring fresh hopes and joys
to you.   —*Mansell*

January 26

Ruling a big country is like cooking a small fish. Too much han-
dling will spoil it.   —*Lao Tzu*

February 26

A man is as good as he has to be, and a woman as bad as she dares.
                                                   —*Elbert Hubbard*

March 26

One of the greatest pieces of economic wisdom is to know what you
do not know.   —*John Kenneth Galbraith*

April 26

All the reasonings of men are not worth one sentiment of women.
                                                   —*Voltaire*

May 26

A community is like a ship; everyone ought to be prepared to take the helm. —*Henrik Ibsen*

June 22

The best way to please one half of the world is not to mind what the other half says. —*Oliver Goldsmith*

July 18

The time to stop talking is when the other person nods his head affirmatively but says nothing. —*Henry S. Haskins*

August 26

When you have to make a choice and don't make it, that is in itself a choice. —*William James*

September 26

Anything that is worth knowing one practically teaches oneself, and the rest obtrudes itself sooner or later. —*Saki*

October 26

The future influences the present just as much as the past.
—*Friedrich Wilhelm Nietzsche*

November 26

The mind attracted by what is false has no relish for better things.
—*Horace*

December 26

Every man has a right to his opinion, but no man has a right to be wrong in his facts. —*Bernard Baruch*

January 27

Love is a pleasing folly; ambition is a serious stupidity.
—*Nicolas Chamfort*

February 27

Sparrows who emulate peacocks are likely to break a thigh.
—*Burmese proverb*

March 27

The best way to get on in the world is to make people believe it's to their advantage to help you. —*Jean de la Bruyère*

April 28

When the blind lead the blind, no wonder they both fall into matrimony. —*George Farquhar*

May 27

We must constantly build dikes of courage to hold back the flood of fear.   *—Martin Luther King, Jr.*

June 23

Friendship is the shadow of the evening, which strengthens with the setting sun of life.   *—Jean de la Fontaine*

July 21

A good listener is not only popular everywhere, but after a while he knows something.   *—Wilson Mizner*

August 23

By persisting in your path, though you forfeit the little, you gain the great.   *—Ralph Waldo Emerson*

September 18

The trouble with most of us is that we would rather be ruined by praise than saved by criticism.   *—Norman Vincent Peale*

October 30

The form in which man experiences the reality of his values is pleasure.   *—Ayn Rand*

November 27

The craving for experience is the beginning of illusion.
     —Jiddu Krishnamurti

December 27

The future has a habit of suddenly and dramatically becoming the present.   *—Roger Babson*

January 30

Anyone who keeps the ability to see beauty never grows old.
     —Franz Kafka

February 4

A banker is a fellow who lends you his umbrella when the sun is shining and wants it back the minute it begins to rain.   *—Mark Twain*

March 31

The measure of a man's real character is what he would do if he knew he never would be found out.   *—Thomas Babington Macaulay*

April 17

Money is like a sixth sense without which you cannot make a complete use of the other five.   *—W. Somerset Maugham*

May 16

Tact is the interpreter of all riddles, the surmounter of all difficulties, the remover of all obstacles. —*William Scargill*

June 28

There are several good protections against temptation, but the surest is cowardice. —*Mark Twain*

July 29

To become a spectator of one's own life is to escape the suffering of life. —*Oscar Wilde*

August 28

Most of us can, as we choose, make this world either a palace or a prison. —*John Lubbock*

September 28

To be able to fill leisure intelligently is the last product of civilization. —*Bertrand Russell*

October 28

Those that think it permissible to tell white lies soon grow colorblind. —*Austin O'Malley*

November 28

The surest way not to fail is to determine to succeed. —*Richard Brinsley Sheridan*

December 28

One cannot be envious and happy at the same time. —*Henry Greber*

January 29

There are three ingredients in the good life: learning, earning and yearning. —*Christopher Morley*

February 18

There is no cure for birth or death except to enjoy the interval. —*George Santayana*

March 29

No one ever became thoroughly bad in one step. —*Juvenal*

April 29

If a man could have half his wishes, he would double his troubles. —*Benjamin Franklin*

May 29

Good fortune, like ripe fruit, ought to be enjoyed while it is present. —*Epictetus*

June 19

To be what we are, and to become what we are capable of becoming, is the only end of life. —*Robert Louis Stevenson*

July 30

A private sin is not so prejudicial in the world as a public indecency. —*Miguel de Cervantes*

August 20

The mystery of life is not a problem to be solved; it is a reality to be experienced. —*Van der Leeuw*

September 29

Sometimes it is more important to discover what one cannot do than what one can do. —*Lin Yutang*

October 29

Pay what you owe, and you'll know what is your own.
—*Benjamin Franklin*

November 12

All our business in life is with doing; enjoyment and suffering come by themselves. —*Johann Wolfgang von Goethe*

December 29

The reason the way of the transgressor is hard is because it's so crowded. —*Kin Hubbard*

January 28

Most people would succeed in small things if they were not troubled with great ambitions. —*Henry Wadsworth Longfellow*

March 30

Work is the greatest thing in the world, so we should always save some of it for tomorrow. —*Don Herold*

April 30

Absence is to love what wind is to fire; it extinguishes the small, it inflames the great. —*Comte de Bussy-Rabutin*

May 25

When we are planning for posterity, we ought to remember that virtue is not hereditary. —*Thomas Paine*

June 30

The magic of first love is our ignorance that it can ever end.
—*Benjamin Disraeli*

July 23

Of all earthly music, that which reaches the farthest into heaven is the beating of a loving heart. *—Henry Ward Beecher*

August 30

In love, there is always one who kisses and one who offers the cheek. *—French proverb*

September 30

Life is made up of sobs, sniffles and smiles, with sniffles predominating. *—William Sydney Porter*

October 27

Knowledge is power only if a man knows what facts not to bother about. *—Robert Lynd*

November 30

Successful savers are straight-thinking spenders. *—Harvey A. Blodgett*

December 30

Life is a succession of lessons which must be lived to be understood. *—Ralph Waldo Emerson*

January 21

To accomplish great things, we must not only act but also dream, not only plan but also believe. *—Anatole France*

March 28

Not everything that is more difficult is more meritorious. *—St. Thomas Aquinas*

May 30

You can never have a greater or a lesser dominion than over yourself. *—Leonardo da Vinci*

July 31

Happiness is someone to love, something to do, and something to hope for. *—Chinese proverb*

August 21

It's a kind of spiritual snobbery that makes people think they can be happy without money. *—Albert Camus*

October 31

Black cats, swooping bats, and impish goblins green, combine with witches riding brooms to challenge Halloween. *—Anon.*

December 31

The old goes out, but the glad young year comes merrily in tomorrow. Happy New Year! *—Emily Huntingdon Miller*

INDEX